A WORLD BANK COUNTRY STUDY

Lithuania

An Opportunity for Economic Success

Volume 1: Main Report

The World Bank
Washington, D.C.

World Bank Country Studies are among the many reports originally prepared for internal use as part of the continuing analysis by the Bank of the economic and related conditions of its developing member countries and of its dialogues with the governments. Some of the reports are published in this series with the least possible delay for the use of governments and the academic, business and financial, and development communities. The typescript of this paper therefore has not been prepared in accordance with the procedures appropriate to formal printed texts, and the World Bank accepts no responsibility for errors. Some sources cited in this paper may be informal documents that are not readily available.

The findings, interpretations, and conclusions expressed in this paper are entirely those of the author(s) and should not be attributed in any manner to the World Bank, to its affiliated organizations, or to members of its Board of Executive Directors or the countries they represent. The World Bank does not guarantee the accuracy of the data included in this publication and accepts no responsibility for any consequence of their use. The boundaries, colors, denominations, and other information shown on any map in this volume do not imply on the part of the World Bank Group any judgment on the legal status of any territory or the endorsement or acceptance of such boundaries.

The material in this publication is copyrighted. Requests for permission to reproduce portions of it should be sent to the Office of the Publisher at the address shown in the copyright notice above. The World Bank encourages dissemination of its work and will normally give permission promptly and, when the reproduction is for noncommercial purposes, without asking a fee. Permission to copy portions for classroom use is granted through the Copyright Clearance Center, Inc., Suite 910, 222 Rosewood Drive, Danvers, Massachusetts 01923, U.S.A.

The cover illustration is *The Mechanism* (1996) by Klaudijus Petrulis, reproduced courtesy of the artist and Regimantas Skaržaukas. Photograph by Rimantas Ivoška.

ISSN: 0253-2123

Library of Congress Cataloging-in-Publication Data

Lithuania : an opportunity for economic success.
      p.   cm. — (A World Bank country study)
  Contents: v. 1. Main report — v. 2. Analytical background.
  ISBN 0-8213-4244-4 (v. 1). — ISBN 0-8213-4327-0 (v. 2)
  1. Lithuania—Economic policy—1991–   2. Lithuania—Economic conditions—1991–   I. World Bank. II. Series.
HC340.6.L565   1998
338.94793—DC21

                                            98-23755
                                            CIP

CONTENTS

Preface

This report has been prepared by a World Bank team composed of Marcelo Giugale (team leader), Dana Cook (banking), Peter Kelly (energy), Jorge Martinez (municipal finance), William Meyers (agriculture), James Welch (privatization), Barbara Lee (infrastructure privatization), Peter Modeen (corporate governance, commercial judicial systems, private investors' perceptions), Ken Messere (tax administration), David Lindeman (pensions), Christopher Bender (pensions), Robert Pardy (securities markets), John Dawson (flow of funds), and Zhicheng Li (macro projections).

Valuable inputs and guidance were received from the following sector specialists at the Bank's Eastern Europe and Central Asia Vice-Presidency: Rodrigo Chaves, Csaba Csaki, Alexander Fleming, Louise Fox, Kristin Gilbertson, Philip Goldman, Marc Heitner, John Holsen, Vilija Kostelnikiene, Mantas Nocius, and Yoshine Uchimura. Useful comments from Ardo Hansson, Robert Holzmann, Dominique Lallement, Laszlo Lovei, Melinda Roth-Alexandrowicz, and Helen Sutch are gratefully acknowledged. Waleed Malik, Gary Stuggins, Samuel Talley, and Dimittri Vittas were the peer reviewers. Dagney Faulk and Midori Makino provided research assistance.

The report was carried out under the general direction of Basil Kavalsky and Pradeep Mitra. James Q. Harrison and Frank Lysy were the senior advisers to the report team.

The editorial staff, coordinated by Michael Geller and Marinette Guevara, included Armanda Carcani, Omar Hadi, David Robbins, and Jessica Rodriguez. Caroline McEuen was the principal editor.

The team wants to express its gratitude to the many officials and institutions in the Lithuanian government, academia, and business community whose cooperation made this report possible. In particular, special thanks are due the staff of the Bank of Lithuania; the Ministries of Agriculture and Forestry, European Integration, Finance, National Economy, Justice, and Social Security and Labor; the Auditing and Accounting Institute; the Lithuanian Securities Commission; the National Stock Exchange; the Central Depository; and the Judicial Training Center, all of whom provided extensive comments to early drafts of this report.

Abstract

Lithuania could now consolidate and complete the achievements of its first structural adjustment effort, create an environment that will allow private entrepreneurs to thrive, and—within five years—become both the fastest-growing economy in the region and a sought-after, successful partner in Europe. In other words, *Lithuania does not have an immediate development problem—it has a unique development opportunity.*

For the country to make the most of that opportunity, this report proposes a policy agenda driven by two overarching objectives: the elimination of the remaining structural sources of macroeconomic imbalance and the rapid shifting of boundaries between the private and the public sectors—both in production and in investment and saving—as means to instill efficiency and to move the country to a higher long-term growth plateau.

To achieve the first objective, policymakers must end the direct and indirect fiscal drains associated with the resolution of pending banking problems, inefficient performance in state-controlled energy companies, poor municipal finance, and the remaining distortions in the agriculture sector. In other words, the first target of the new reform agenda should be to do away—permanently—with the operating deficit of the "quasi-public" sector (that is, the aggregate financial performance of the general government, the public energy sector, strategic public enterprises, farmers, pensioners, and the other sectors and interest groups that are, in effect, financially dependent on the state).

The second target of the new reform agenda—an efficiency-led increase in long-term growth—will require reforms in the legal, regulatory, and institutional frameworks, not only for privatization and private sector initiative, but also for the operation of the pension system and the development of the securities market. The core idea behind this element of the agenda is to place the allocation of the country's resources fully in the charge of profit-driven, private initiative. Freed to accumulate and invest their own long-term savings, private owners should, through their dealings in the securities market, put increased pressure on the managers of private and newly privatized firms to perform. The ensuing efficiency gains should bring the economy onto a faster growth path.

LITHUANIA–FISCAL YEAR

January 1–December 31

CURRENCY EQUIVALENTS

(as of 20 April 1998)

Currency Unit	=	Litas
4 Litai	=	US$1

WEIGHTS AND MEASURES

Metric System

ABREVIATIONS AND ACRONYMS

ADR	American Depository Receipt	LPC	Lithuania Power Company
BFTA	Baltic Free Trade Agreement	LPG	Liquefied petroleum gas
BNM	Basic nontaxable minimum	MCF	Municipal Credit Facility
BoL	Bank of Lithuania	MEA	Minister of European Affairs
BSD	Bank Supervision Department	MFN	Most-favored nation
CAA	Court Administration Agency	MMPP	Minimal marginal purchase price
CEEC	Central and eastern European countries	MPARLA	Ministry of Public Reform and Local Authorities
CEFTA	Central European Free Trade Association	MoAF	Ministry of Agriculture and Forestry
CHP	Combined heat and power	MoJ	Ministry of Justice
CIS	Commonwealth of Independent States	MSL	Minimum Subsistence Level
CIT	Corporation income tax	MSSL	Ministry of Social Security and Labor
CSDL	Central Securities Depository	mtoe	Million tons of oil equivalent
DCF	Discounted cash flow method	MVV	Mannheimer Versorgungs-und Verkehrsgesellschaft NGH
DH	District heating		
DOD	Debt outstanding and disbursed	MW	Mega-watt
EFTA	European Free Trade Association	NAP	National Agricultural Program
EPC	Energy Pricing Commission	NDC	National Defined Contribution Accounts
ESR	Energy sector review	NOCs	Notional Defined Contribution Accounts
EBRD	European Bank for Reconstruction and Development	NSEL	National Stock Exchange of Lithuania
		OECD	Organization for Economic Cooperation and Development
EU	European Union		
FDI	Foreign direct investment	PADP	Private Agricultural Development Program
FSU	Former Soviet Union	PAYGO	Pay as you go
GAO	Gross agricultural output	PIT	Personal income tax
GATT	General Agreement on Tariffs and Trade	PJ	Petajoules
Gcal	Giga-calorie	PPP	Purchasing power parity
GDP	Gross domestic product	PSD	Private sector development
GDR	Global Depository Receipt	PSEs	Producer Subsidy Equivalents
GoL	Government of Lithuania	RSF	Rural Support Fund
HOB	Heat-only boiler	SAL	Structural Adjustment Loan
IAS	International accounting standards	SEM	Small and medium-size
ICOR	Incremental capital output ratio	SODRA	Social Insurance Fund
IEA	International Energy Agency	SRP	Savings Restitution Plan
IFC	International Finance Corporation	TB	Treasury bills
INPP	Ignalina Nuclear Power Plant	Tcal	Tetra-calorie
IPO	Initial public offering	TMCF	Transitional Municipal Credit Facility
IPS	Interconnected Power System	TOE	Tons of oil equivalent
ISA	International Standards on Audit	Twh	Tetra-watt
KLASC	Klaipeda Stevedoring	UNDP	United Nations Development Program
ktoe	Thousand tons of oil equivalent	USAID	United States Agency for International Development
Kwh	Kilowatt		
LAAI	Lithuanian Auditing and Accounting Institute	VAT	Value added tax
LG	Lithuania Gas Company	VICA	Vilnius International Commercial Arbitration
LIA	Lithuanian Investment Agency	WTO	World Trade Organization
LISCO	Lithuanian Shipping	XGS	Exports of goods and nonfactor services
LLA	Lithuania Lawyers Association		

—for The World Bank—	
Vice President:	Johannes Linn, ECAVP
PREM Director:	Pradeep Mitra, ECSPE
Chief Economist:	Marcelo Selowsky, ECAVP
Country Director:	Basil Kavalsky, ECC09
Sector Leader:	Frank Lysy, ECSPE
Senior Adviser:	James Q. Harrison, ECSPE
Team Leader:	Marcelo Giugale, ECSPE

LITHUANIA
A OPPORTUNITY FOR ECONOMIC SUCCESS

Background and Rationale

Soon after its declaration of independence, Lithuania launched a program of market-based economic reforms that has thus far achieved remarkable results. Price liberalization, voucher privatization, trade opening, legal reform, institutional development, and enhancement of the social safety net are either being implemented or are already in place. Policies in the real sector were initially underpinned by a front-loaded stabilization effort: a currency board was introduced, financial markets were freed, the capital account was thrown open, and fiscal deficits were brought under control.

In early 1996, however, a second generation of transition issues emerged that threatened both the reform results already achieved and the medium-term growth prospects of the country. A banking crisis erupted in January of that year, driven by a combination of ineffective bank supervision, poor banking practices, and deep-rooted sectoral imbalances. The government acted decisively to address those problems. With support from a US$80 million Structural Adjustment Loan (SAL) from the World Bank, the authorities embarked on a broad economic reform program with two immediate objectives: the resolution of the banking system's operational and undercapitalization problems, and a reduction in the most severe imbalances in three key sectors of the economy (energy, agriculture, and social insurance), imbalances that contributed to the erosion of bank capital.

With the short-term situation under control, there is now an urgent need to define a successor policy agenda. That urgency arises not because the Lithuanian economy is stagnant (it is growing apace) or because inflation is excessively high (it has recently reached single digits), but because Lithuania is currently faced with a major policy choice. The country could refrain from faster and deeper structural reform, resort to short-term tools to finance remaining sectoral imbalances, achieve moderate growth and relative price stability for a time, and bid for external assistance to enter the European Union (EU) after its Baltic neighbors and to survive the competition of the single market. Alternatively, Lithuania could now decisively consolidate and complete the many achievements of its first structural adjustment effort, rapidly create an environment that will allow private entrepreneurs to thrive, and—within five years— become one of the fastest-growing economies in the region and a sought-after, successful partner in Europe. In other words, *Lithuania does not have an immediate development problem—it has a unique development opportunity.*

This report explores avenues that will allow Lithuania to make the most of this opportunity. It has been written by a World Bank team at the request of the government and has been financed by a Japanese PHRD grant (as part of the preparation for a possible successor SAL operation) and by the Canadian, Finnish, and Irish Trust Funds at the World Bank.

The report is composed of two volumes. Volume I distills findings and conclusions and builds a Policy Action Plan for fast, stable growth. Volume II contains a collection of twelve Policy Notes that provide the technical analysis behind that plan. While the Notes are sector-specific in nature, they are dominated by two overarching objectives: the elimination of the remaining structural sources of macroeconomic imbalance, and the rapid shifting of boundaries between the private and the public sectors—both in production and in investment and saving—as means to instill efficiency and to move the country to a higher long-term growth plateau. Achieving these two objectives will directly facilitate reaching a third goal, one of critical importance for Lithuania: accession to the EU.

To achieve the first objective, policymakers must end the direct and indirect fiscal drains associated with the resolution of pending banking problems, inefficient performance in state-controlled energy companies, poor municipal finance, and the remaining distortions in the agriculture sector. In other words, the first target of the new reform agenda should be to do away—permanently—with the operating deficit of the "quasi-public" sector (that is, the aggregate financial performance of the general government, the public energy sector, strategic public enterprises, farmers, pensioners, and the other sectors and interest groups that are, in effect, financially dependent on the state). That deficit has been preliminarily estimated to be three to four times higher than the posted financial deficit in the general government accounts (and roughly equal to the country's money base).[1]

Further, the authorities' recent announcement of the phased dismantling of the currency board arrangement (prompted by a medium-term desire to join the European Monetary Union) has made the elimination of the quasi-public deficit a much more pressing objective, because imbalances in state-dependent sectors could then put pressure on money creation, and thus jeopardize Lithuania's price stability.

The second target of the new reform agenda—an efficiency-led increase in long-term growth—will require reforms in the legal, regulatory, and institutional frameworks, not only for privatization and private sector initiative, but also for the operation of the pension system and the development of the securities market. The core idea behind this element of the agenda would be to place the allocation of the country's resources fully in the charge of profit-driven, private initiative. Freed to accumulate and invest their own long-term savings, private owners should, through their dealings in the securities market, put increased pressure on the managers of private and newly privatized firms to perform. The ensuing efficiency gains should bring the economy onto a faster growth path.

It should be noted at the outset that the collection of sectoral policy notes and policy recommendations presented in this report is not meant to be exhaustive. Rather than covering all relevant sectors and issues, it focuses on those that, at the margin, are considered a priority for the Lithuanian policymakers.

The Main Remaining Sources of Quasi-Public-Sector Deficit

The State's Role in Banking

Although the immediate effects of the 1996 crisis have passed, Lithuania's banking system is still undergoing adjustment. Profits from early-transition sources (artificially high spreads on lending, primarily to finance trading with former Soviet Union countries) have declined significantly, as has the number of operating banks (primarily through failures). There are also indications of intrabank consolidation (for example, rationalization of branch networks and staffing) among the remaining market

---

1. See M. Giugale, "Lithuania: Macroeconomic Issues and Prospects for a Transition Country at a Junction" (prepared for Lithuania's Agricultural Strategy Workshop, April, Washington, D.C., 1997, processed).

participants. The legal and regulatory frameworks have been vastly improved, as has the capacity of the Bank of Lithuania (BoL) to enforce them. International accounting standards and more stringent supervisory rules have been adopted. A partially funded deposit insurance system is now in place. Nevertheless, the sector still faces a core challenge that, if unattended, will likely put renewed pressure on the government to act as "compensator of last resort"—the role of the state in banking has not fully changed from that of self-serving owner to that of independent regulator. This manifests itself in at least four weak aspects of the industry—and in hefty costs to the public purse.[2]

First, political interference in bank lending decisions is still an issue. The BoL's supervisory independence appears limited, given the propensity of the Seimas (with or without government sponsorship) to pass banking-related laws on an ad hoc, bank-specific basis. The special compensation for depositors of the failed Innovation Bank and the effective waiver of the new supervisory rules for two state-controlled banks—both through laws recently passed by the Seimas—are prime examples of that interference. Similarly, the salaries of state bank managers have recently been linked to the civil service pay scale by a unilateral administrative decision of government.

Second, serious capital adequacy and corporate governance problems affect the state-controlled banks (which account for over half of the system's deposits), while their privatization is stalled. One institution (the Savings Bank) holds the largest concentration of individual deposits in the country, is the largest buyer of treasury bills (TBs), and has monopolistic rights to service the state's compensation and restitution schemes. This confluence of power effectively converts the Savings Bank into a potential parallel treasury.

Third, the legal framework for banking activities, albeit improved, remains suboptimal. Banks are not allowed to take title to land, and foreclosure procedures for movable property are extremely cumbersome and lengthy, forcing banks either not to lend or to develop complicated and uncertain alternatives.

Finally, the coinsurance schedules of the deposit insurance system may prove both inadequate to avoid moral hazard and unaffordable within the system's own means, especially given its unspecified legal role in recovering funds from failed banks. Put differently, the state remains effectively liable for unnecessarily generous insurance coverage.

The Energy Sector's Level of Efficiency

Persistent financial deficits in state-controlled energy companies are probably the most serious threat to the stability of Lithuania's fiscal account, and thus to its macroeconomic framework. (All in all, direct and indirect fiscal support to the energy sector's producers and consumers amounts to the equivalent of about 2–3 percent of GDP yearly.) The government has initiated several important reforms in this area. Formal mechanisms to reduce payment arrears have been put in place (and have started to bear fruit), the state has begun to pay its subsidy-related debts to the Lithuanian Power Company (LPC), an independent Energy Pricing Commission (EPC) has been established to oversee cost-recovering pricing, the district heating (DH) network has been decentralized down to the municipal level, and supervisory boards have been appointed at LPC and Lithuanian Gas (LG). The government has publicly indicated its commitment to disengage from the day-to-day operation of its energy companies and has put its oil-related businesses (Lithuanian Oil) on the immediate privatization list.

---

2. The compensations and recapitalizations associated with bank failures in 1996 alone will cost the equivalent of about 3–4 percent of GDP.

The sector's adjustment, however, is far from over. Vast overcapacity still exists in power generation (peak power-generation capacity is three times larger than peak daily demand) and gas distribution (currently operating at about one-quarter of capacity), even though demand (especially from households) has barely begun to adapt to the reality of energy prices that are closer to cost-recovery and world levels. The economy's energy intensity remains three times higher than the Organization of Economic Cooperation and Development (OECD) average. And, because of its outdated technology and neglect of maintenance, the sector faces formidable operational problems (for instance, at current replacement rates, DH in Lithuania will cease to exist within a decade). This poses three broad policy questions: how can municipally owned DH companies be made viable, what role should the government play in power and gas, and how can energy conservation be fostered?

There are good technical, commercial, and managerial reasons for decentralizing DH to the municipal level (and successful international examples of this policy). There is no doubt, however, that Lithuanian municipalities, which have serious financial problems of their own (see the next section), have inherited a problem-riddled asset. First, investment needs are massive. As mentioned earlier, the system's technology is obsolete (the preeminence of the Ignalina Nuclear Power Plant, INPP, resulted in dependence on relatively inefficient, heat-only boilers, rather than combined heat and power plants), heat losses in the distribution network are all but out of control (at almost one-third of supply), flow and temperature controls at substations are lacking, and half of domestic consumers are unmetered. While under the new tariff-setting mechanism, EPC is to approve cost-recovering price levels that will allow for needed long-term investment, the financing mechanisms for such investments are simply not in place; they will take time to develop; and they will very likely engage the finances of the local and central governments (that is, it is extremely improbable that the DH companies will be able to borrow directly or without guarantees). Second, the enforceability of the new tariff system remains untested. Political pressure from local constituencies and the impossibility of cutting off electricity to defaulting heat customers are likely to undermine payment discipline, especially among sister municipally owned organizations (who have the worst paying record of all DH clients). Third, the competitive position of DH will weaken over the next few years. With recent tariff increases of up to 40 percent (and in some cases higher), switching to electric and gas heating will accelerate, especially as consumer subsidies are phased out or are delivered as direct income support. The core issue is how to raise tariffs high enough to cover economic cost levels (that is, including capital depreciation and formation), while ensuring that customers will indeed pay. Finally, the new DH companies still lack the needed corporate governance structures (perhaps in the form of supervisory boards) to ensure adequate management performance. The absence of basic business plans is a telling result of this flaw.

The problems described above will seriously challenge the viability of DH companies (and the finances of their municipal owners). Some will not be able to cope, and corporate failures are not unthinkable. This need not be a negative outcome: competition by private sources of supply could fill the supply gap in a more efficient way, and at a lower cost to the economy as a whole.

Changing the role of the state from owner to regulator in the power and gas industries is the second key energy-related issue that the Lithuanian authorities will need to address in the medium term. Three problems, however, stand in the way of that change. First, efficient regulation of the electricity market is all but impossible, especially at the generation level, because of the lack of transparency in the accounts of LPC and INPP. The former has only recently begun to produce accounts under international standards, and its true relative cost structure remains unknown; the latter simply faces (or follows) no information disclosure requirements. And neither of the two meets EU directives for the internal market in electricity (for instance, in their accounts). Second, there is no strategy for, or built-in incentive toward, the privatization of LPC and LG. In the case of LPC, the timing, the method, the possibility of separate sales of electricity generation assets, the number of regionally based electricity distribution companies to be created, the market mechanism for power trading, and the destination of proceeds from the sale of ancillary activities are all to be decided. The situation is worse for LG. Its privatization seems to have fallen into a policy vacuum, not least because it has been effectively left to the company's own management to decide and implement. Third, the mechanisms to ensure that both companies are run efficiently until privatization are not in place. Their supervisory boards, appointed in 1997, are not yet operative (some company managers report that they are unaware of their nominal existence), and the salaries of senior executives remain linked to the civil service pay scale. Not surprisingly, both are underperforming enterprises (they both posted losses in 1996) and have no articulated cost rationalization plans (despite being grossly overstaffed by international standards).

Finally, energy conservation is the third major policy issue that will dominate the long-term adjustment of Lithuania's energy sector. The Soviet legacy of energy profligacy will take time to disappear. If only half of the estimated potential annual energy saving from conservation were realized, the country would have no need for its nuclear power plant (INPP). Fortunately, apart from the more cost-sensitive pricing mechanisms mentioned earlier, good energy-saving initiatives have been launched by the recently established Energy Conservation Program, especially in demand-side public awareness (for a good reason—in a recent survey, almost half of householders interviewed thought energy conservation was a waste of time or had no opinion). The program's operation, however, is hampered by two major problems. On the one hand, the state has yet to pay its planned funding contribution. On the other hand, a fifth of the potential energy saving mentioned above is based on correcting inefficiency in the very state-owned enterprises that control Lithuania's energy sector.

Uncertainty in Municipal Finances

The rationalization and modernization of the system of municipal finances will play a critical role in placing Lithuania's quasi-public accounts on a sustainable path. Close to a third of the consolidated government's spending is at the municipal level; key public services such as public utilities, education, health, and social protection are primarily the responsibility of municipal governments; and, as explained above, local authorities now own the DH system. Local governments have a comparative advantage in the provision of these basic services because they are closer to the beneficiaries and are better able to determine the combination and levels of service that fit local priorities and willingness to pay. But with no formal taxing power as exists in fiscally decentralized systems, and with no clear borrowing guidelines,[3] the municipalities' financial balance is of prime concern to the stability of the country's macroeconomic framework because the central government implicitly plays the role of funder of last resort. The lack of formal taxing powers has also left local governments in a position in which they cannot make needed investments in infrastructure or increase their creditworthiness.

In July 1997, a Law on Methodology for Establishing Municipal Budget Income was enacted that does much to address the perverse incentives and uncertainties that have plagued the country's system of municipal finances during the transition years. But the reform remains incomplete, and in some areas is flawed. This leads to a level of uncertainty that renders municipal budgets virtually impossible to predict and manage, and it creates a major potential liability for the central government. This acute predictability problem affects the three main budget areas—expenditures, revenues, and financing.

---

3. A decree on borrowing by local authorities was passed on April 28, 1998, but it needs to be followed by legislation and detailed guidelines.

Municipal expenditure assignments remain unsettled. On the one hand, unfunded mandates from the central government to municipalities are a common practice, one that is contrary to the letter of the above-mentioned law. On the other hand, responsibility for capital investment remains undetermined, a critical problem given the lack of infrastructure maintenance observed at the local level during the past five years (municipalities are, in principle, responsible for investments related to the services assigned to them, while at the same time the central government is responsible for investment above Lt 5 million). In addition, while decentralizing DH will likely lead to badly needed improvements in management and organization, it is clear that the municipalities are now responsible for a service that has been plagued by low tariffs, low collection rates, obsolete equipment and acute investment needs, large operating losses, and heavy debt burdens.

Municipalities continue to enjoy no revenue autonomy because they cannot raise their own taxes, modify the rates of taxes with centrally shared proceeds (notably, the personal income tax), or foresee their revenue shares (which are set by Seimas on a year-by-year basis) with sufficient accuracy. This lack of autonomy—and certainty—is not helped by the supplementary system of equalization transfers from the central budget established in July 1997. Although remarkably advanced and elaborated, this scheme leaves too many distributional parameters to be decided by Seimas on a yearly basis.

Finally, there is no legal framework to regulate municipal borrowing, and no market mechanisms for its operation. Such borrowing is made even more difficult by weak local budgeting processes, which render municipalities unable to present creditworthy accounts.

The Unfinished Reforms in Agriculture

At the beginning of 1997, the Lithuanian government began implementing a better-targeted, more transparent, more cost-effective, and less distorting support system for farms and rural communities. These reforms have set a new direction for agricultural and rural policy, one that is more market-friendly and provides an improved framework for longer-term reforms and investments—something the sector needed badly, especially in light of the prospects for accession to the EU. Equally important, the reforms were a recognition that the agricultural sector's level of financial dependency on the state (roughly estimated at the equivalent of 1–2 percent of GDP annually) was no longer sustainable. Thus, the authorities eliminated or reduced the levels of subsidies and support prices and targeted direct payments to higher-quality products; the value added tax (VAT) preferential rate for domestically produced food and agricultural products was discontinued; and subsidized credit programs were replaced with targeted investment grants, a Rural Credit Guarantee Fund, and a copayment system for interest on short-term bank loans for fuel, fertilizer, and chemicals.

While the initial, massive adjustment to the new market realities is nearly over, several policy-driven tasks inherent in building a financially viable, competitive agriculture and food sector remain to be accomplished. Completion of these tasks is crucial if the sector is not to revert to, and deepen, its financial dependency on the state. First, the land restitution process needs to be completed. At present, only about half of the agricultural land has transparent private ownership. The legal framework for restitution has been subject to repeated amendments, the last of which, while participatory in nature, will delay the process even further because it both opens new opportunities for original landowners to make claims and provides for cash compensation options, even though fiscal resources are not readily available. At current restitution rates, and under optimistic assumptions, the restitution process will take another five years to complete. This slow resolution, in combination with the prohibition of landownership by domestic legal persons and upper limits on the size of the land owned by individuals, has delayed the emergence of a functioning land market. Lack of such a market has, in turn, hindered the development of agricultural credit (because land becomes poor-quality collateral) and the consolidation of the country's highly atomized landholdings into more efficient, larger farms. Second, while the vast majority of agro-enterprises are currently private, the privatization process has not attracted significant foreign investment to the agriculture sector, and the badly needed technological and management upgrading that comes with it.

Third, although sound progress has been achieved in the rationalization of agricultural support mechanisms, the process is still incomplete. Minimum prices have been reduced, the budget for direct subsidies has been drastically cut, product eligibility has been curtailed, and credit subsidies have been essentially discontinued. These changes still leave Lithuania with three times the level of producer subsidy equivalents found in Estonia and Latvia (but only about one-third of the EU rate, and slightly below the OECD average). The remaining support blurs market signals for farmers, and it remains subject to political manipulation. Similarly, agriculture enjoys a preferential tax regime. Individual farmers are exempt from income tax, and agricultural enterprises face rates that are one-third the level of their nonagricultural counterparts. The weighted average agricultural import tariff, albeit greatly reduced from its early-transition level, is still about 30 percent.[4]

Fourth, the state needs a strategy to address the country's forthcoming integrated rural development challenge. Since independence, agriculture's share in GDP has remained stagnant, while its employment grew by about a fifth, even though its average wages were (and are) well below the average in the economy. This illustrates the role the sector has played as an early-transition social safety net (certainly aided by the generous land restitution process). As the sector's adjustment takes hold, support is rationalized, and primary agriculture becomes more efficient, much of that safety net will disappear. The difficulties presented by the coming changes will be worsened by the legacy of relative neglect of rural infrastructure inherited from the Soviet era, especially neglect of the financial infrastructure.

Finally, as the role of the state in agriculture changed from directing the sector through central plans to providing a framework conducive to its market-driven operation, the functions, budget, and skill requirements of the related civil service also changed. This has created an acute need for continuing development of the agriculture-related institutions of government, as well as for public resources to deliver externality-capturing services (for example, extension services and statistical information systems that conform to EU standards).

Key Impediments to a Private-Sector-Led Increase in Efficiency and Growth

Lithuania could, in a relatively short period of time, reach much higher levels of efficiency in the utilization of its limited resources. On the one hand, about one-third of the country's GDP is still produced under the management incentives of the civil service rather than those of profit-driven enterprises, while important impediments in the country's business environment continue to inhibit private initiative in producing the other two-thirds. On the other hand, the state continues to be in charge of allocating retirement saving (worth about 6 percent of GDP annually). A combination of privatization, a better business climate, and funded pension reform thus has the power to upgrade efficiency in Lithuania. More important, these reforms will drive, and be facilitated by, further development of the securities markets in which retirement savings will be invested and newly private firms traded. That development can substantially add to the pattern of increased efficiency because improved mechanisms for asset pricing will facilitate better decisionmaking in private saving and investment.

---

4. Excluding sugar, which has an import tariff of 87 percent.

There are clearly important synergies among privatization (and, more generally, improvement in the private business environment), pension reform, and securities market development that policymakers can exploit to raise overall allocative efficiency, put the economy on a much higher growth path, and, as mentioned earlier, place Lithuania in a stronger position to enter and compete in the EU. The analysis summarized below (and the policy recommendations presented later) seek to capture these synergies.

The Incentive Framework for Rapid Privatization

Lithuania had a voucher privatization program from 1991 to 1995 that resulted in the total or partial privatization of 5,700 primarily small and medium-size enterprises. As is common with voucher privatizations, Lithuania's experience left an important legacy of residual government ownership in many privatized firms, and it effectively favored incumbent insiders. In many instances this led to poor corporate governance and limited access to capital for the privatized firms. By and large, Lithuania's initial privatization effort, while effective in creating public support for market reforms, failed to fully bring about the efficiency gains that private ownership should entail. The government also launched a cash privatization program under the 1995 Law on Privatization of State-Owned and Municipal Property, with uninspiring results—through July 1997, the program had only realized about US$20.2 million in proceeds. Because of its shortcomings, that law was replaced in December 1997. The new legislation, however, while a modest improvement, stills falls short of providing a means for rapid privatization. The central problem is that the law fails to set up the right incentive structure for the many players involved in the sale process. As those incentives stand today, privatization is unlikely to happen, except for unsystematic, ad hoc efforts by the highest levels of government (such as the ongoing privatization of telecommunications). There are three main reasons for this.

First, the law does not state in aggregate terms what should be sold, or by what time. While it centralizes the ownership of all state assets into a purpose-built State Property Fund, and away from the vested interests of line ministries, it does not explicitly mark assets for sale, even in the medium and long term. These oversights weaken the commitment and urgency of the privatization effort.

Second, the mandate of the State Property Fund is to manage and administer all of the state's assets, not necessarily to sell them. Without an explicit duty to sell (or any parallel incentive, such as the revenue-collection targets of a Ministry of Finance), it is improbable that the fund will seek to solve the outstanding implementation problem hampering the privatization process, including insufficient institutional capacity, reluctance to use qualified advisers (especially on a success-fee basis), insistence on outdated valuation methods, and overall lack of perceived commitment to the process (losing both the confidence-building effect of actual privatizations on foreign investors and the efficiency-enhancing effect of expected sales on public enterprise managers). Equally important, without a law that explicitly calls for privatization, the managers of the State Property Fund will have no reason to assume the risk of personal liability arising from the probability of mishandled sales.

Third, many of Lithuania's state assets are infrastructure-related and require special preparation before they are suitable for privatization. That preparation has just begun. Horizontal and vertical restructuring will likely be needed in the power sector (to break up generation, transmission, and distribution activities and to allow for competition at the generation and distribution levels). The details of the regulatory framework (pricing, standards, investment, and the like) in sectors where competition will not be feasible are yet to be determined. And, while a Concessions Law has been put in place to allow for nondivestiture forms of private participation, it has not yet been tested, either at the central or the local level of government.

Second-Generation Constraints to Private Sector Development

Lithuania's privatization, and the economywide efficiency enhancement that it is expected to prompt, will not materialize if the overall framework for private business remains inadequate. The World Bank's 1995 *Lithuania—Private Sector Report* identified (based, inter alia, on a survey of enterprises) a series of constraints to private sector development (PSD) in the country, especially in the areas of regulation, barriers to market entry, tax, and customs administration. This study led to policy reform efforts that, while not yet fully implemented, have substantially improved Lithuania's business environment. For example, technical assistance for title, mortgage, and lien registration is under way; foreign banks are now allowed to operate, and do operate, in the domestic market; nonagricultural landownership rights have been extended to foreign firms; promotion of foreign investment has been placed high on the government's declared policy agenda; and the customs department is now being reformed (and placed under much closer scrutiny).

Nevertheless, an array of second-generation PSD constraints is becoming apparent as the transition process unfolds. In the preparation of this report, an update of the 1995 enterprise survey mentioned above was carried out, in conjunction with a large array of interviews with incumbent and potential domestic and foreign entrepreneurs in Lithuania. Three key areas of constraint stand out from a public policy point of view—tax administration, the commercial judicial system, and corporate governance.[5]

The approach to *tax administration* in Lithuania is less than business-friendly. While tax rates (especially VAT and the tax on corporate income) are not very different from the OECD norms, Lithuania's actual collection structure relies much more heavily on indirect taxes, mainly because of the numerous concessions built into the system and the low level of individual compliance. These two factors are symptomatic of the overall problem of the country's system of administering taxes—its arbitrariness. Lithuanian taxpayers have neither independent appeal mechanisms outside the court system (which, as explained below, faces serious problems of its own) nor a guiding, legally enforced accounting standard (effectively turning tax audits into tax assessments) to assist them. This grants formidable power to the individual tax inspectors and makes taxpayers more inclined to accept (and, indeed, to seek) informal settlements. Both the quality of the business climate and tax revenue suffer as a result. The problem is compounded by persistent institutional efficiency problems at the tax inspectorate itself (low remuneration; lack of staff manuals; lack of synchronization among tax, customs, and social security authorities; an excessive number of local tax offices; almost universal auditing techniques; and so forth).

The status of the *commercial judicial system* is the second key constraint to PSD in Lithuania. While the speed at which the system abandoned its Soviet legacy has been impressive (current clearance rates, backlogs, and waiting times are not drastically different from those of several western European countries), it has not yet fully adapted to the needs of a modern market economy. Thus far, the problem is the quality (not the quantity) and the accessibility of court services.

Quality is hampered by three main factors. First, there is an acute shortage of qualified judges. The issue is not the number of judges (the ratio of judges for each million citizens is higher in Lithuania than in France or Belgium), but rather the mismatch between their skills and the growing demand for the

---

5. During the survey and interviews, several other areas of constraint emerged, but not all of these are—or should be—the focus of public policymaking because they represent claims for larger rents by incumbent entrepreneurs (for example, through lower taxation, greater protection from import competition, lower interest rates on credit, and so forth). Thus, these areas are not addressed in this report.

market-oriented legal expertise that an emerging private sector in transition requires. This is less the result of unattractive remuneration (the average salary gap between judges and private sector lawyers is proportionally smaller than in many western European countries) than of the speed at which the existing education system, itself in transition, can turn out suitable professionals. The quality problem generated by the judges' skill base is compounded by a shortage of court support personnel (the ratio of such personnel to judges in Lithuania is one-sixth of the ratio in Portugal, for example); cumbersome court procedures run with an inadequate physical infrastructure and weak enforcement tools (there is only about one bailiff for each judge); and the effective lack of alternative dispute-resolution mechanisms, court-associated or private (a relatively acceptable legal and institutional framework for arbitration has only recently been put in place). The second main factor hampering the quality of court services is the quality of the body of law itself. At best, Lithuanian laws are difficult to interpret, both because they are the result of myriad, necessarily rushed, enactment efforts in the aftermath of independence and because the legislative process remains less than efficient (participation is limited; drafting and harmonization are done by an understaffed department of Seimas; implementing decrees are issued with delay, and sometimes not issued at all; and Seimas frequently approves draft laws after modifying them in substance without consultation with the drafting team). Finally, it is of critical importance that the quality of the court services, and of the internal initiatives to improve them, is limited by a judiciary that is independent in principle but not in practice—budget and personnel decisions remain prerogatives of the Ministry of Justice.

Quality considerations are clearly one element that weakens the support provided to private business activity by Lithuania's judicial system. The other is the system's limited accessibility, which is caused by its inefficient pricing. Claimants currently have to pay, up-front, 5 percent of the value of their claims for their cases to be heard in court in first instance, irrespective of the court's hearing costs, and under the usually unfulfilled expectation that a reimbursement judgment for that fee will later be enforced on the losing party.[6] While effective in preventing frivolous charges, the financial burden on the claimant implied by this pricing arrangement acts as a major deterrent for enterprises (smaller ones in particular), especially in a country where free legal aid is not available.

Weak mechanisms to exercise effective *corporate governance* is the third critical constraint to PSD identified in this report. After five decades of central planning and six years of transition, Lithuanian enterprise managers, both private and public, are still not subject to the same internal incentives toward profitability (and thus, efficiency) as their counterparts in most developed and emerging market economies. Instead, they operate in an incentive framework conducive to unchecked misappropriation or outright fraud. It is not surprising that the above-mentioned survey of investors' perceptions found that only a quarter of Lithuanian corporate managers believe their shareholders are the main decisionmakers in the major strategic issues that affect their companies, or that management ownership has increased by half since independence. This pervasive manager incentive framework has several causes.

The first cause is the weak legal protection provided to investors. For instance, the Company Law does not explicitly require managers to serve the interest of shareholders first, and it does not include size-specific protections for small investors (for example, a qualified-majority requirement for major corporate decisions). In addition, disclosure requirements (and their enforcement) for companies traded in the stock market are insufficient; legally sanctioned accounting and auditing standards (along the lines of international practices) are still missing; as explained before, the status of the commercial judicial

---

6. Smaller, but still up-front, fees are applied to first appeals and to appeals at the court of cassation.

system is not conducive to challenging corporate managers in court; and, until recently, the legal mechanisms for debt recovery were debtor-friendly (for example, in terms of seniority of collateral-holding creditors in bankruptcy), which has prevented banks from exercising outside pressure on managers (a problem compounded by the lack of domestic credit-rating agencies).

Second, large shareholders or shareholders with substantial minority holdings, especially institutional investors, are rare (apart from the government and management), because voucher-based investment funds all but disappeared after the mass privatization initiative, laws governing the operation of funded pensions are still under design, and reform in the state-dominated insurance market is yet to begin. Third, the legal framework governing the relationship between the board (or boards) of a company and its management is inadequate. This problem is made particularly acute by the failure of the Company Law to specify penalties for withholding information from the board(s) and to include clear provisions for incentive contracts.

Finally, overall corporate governance in Lithuania is weakened by extensive state ownership. Of some 2,000 enterprises with majority or minority state ownership (producing over a third of the country's GDP), some 1,200 are under the State Fund for Securities, which has a staff of ten. The State Fund is being merged into the new State Property Fund, although this is unlikely to improve corporate governance. The state effectively has board representation in only about a tenth of the firms in which it has a stake (mostly in large, infrastructure-related corporations under the jurisdiction of the Ministry of National Economy). This not only suggests a lack of performance pressure on the management of those companies, but also questions the need for keeping them in public hands.

Incomplete Pension Reform

Since the beginning of 1995, Lithuania has been operating a reformed and progressive pay-as-you-go (Paygo) social insurance system.[7] Although Lithuania has one of the most modest pension benefit schemes of the eastern and central European region (with a targeted benefit of 40 percent of the final-year wage for a full-career worker), and thus a relatively low payroll contribution rate (effectively around 24 percent of payroll), the government's early 1997 projections forecast that the system, in its present form, is facing imbalances in the short and medium term—that is, persistent deficits that will be worth about 0.5–1.0 percent of GDP annually by the year 2000. The reason behind these deficits appears to be that, despite Lithuania's curtailment of early retirement privileges, the already legislated increase in retirement ages is not proceeding fast enough to support both the caseload inherited from the old regime and the new entrants of the transition period, in which retirement ages are increasing, at promised benefit levels. As in other countries in the region, Lithuania is also facing compliance problems, which do not seem to be improving. To address these issues under the government's structural adjustment program supported by the SAL, the government drafted legislation to accelerate the increase in retirement ages and to contain the growth of benefits within the envelope of existing resources. That legislation, however, has not been introduced.

In addition, the existing Paygo system needs further improvements to address incentives and long-term imbalances, public understanding of the costs and benefits of the system, and compliance. Further, to assure long-term balance, it appears that retirement ages must be gradually increased to age 65.0 for both genders. Finally, to prevent political pressures from building to increase the Paygo benefit from its relatively modest level, the government should move quickly to enact its already well-drafted

---

7. Social insurance refers here to the old-age, disability, widow(er), survivor, and noncontributory social and state pensions, as well as short-term insurance benefits such as unemployment, maternity, and sickness allowances.

framework law for Private (Nonstate) Pensions and put the necessary resources in place to implement that law. With the exception of the increase in retirement ages to 65, all these measures are also contained in the government's structural reform plan, but have not been translated in all instances into proposed legislation or other needed steps. If these measures were taken, Lithuania would have a pension system that is financially sustainable in the long term.

These modifications to the Paygo system, however desirable, would not cause Lithuania's pension system to contribute to the country's full potential for economic efficiency and growth—that is, help move Lithuania to a high economic growth plateau. In contrast, a movement toward a partially captialized pension system could assist growth in three ways. First, even if balanced, Paygo systems do not allow for the free accumulation and market-driven allocation of individual retirement savings. Successive cohorts have less capital accumulated and cannot become, through the securities market, an expanding class of shareholders who can put performance pressure on corporate sector management. Those positive effects on securities market development and corporate governance, based on the experience in other countries, could generate enough efficiency gains to raise the economy's long-term annual growth rate by 1 percentage point.[8] Second, the existing Paygo carries adverse labor incentives because of its lack of obvious connection between the payroll contribution made by the firms on behalf of workers and the benefits these workers eventually receive. Finally, with a strong private pension system in place, a growing pool of domestic investors would emerge, with a strong interest in seeing the privatization program unfold more rapidly, which could vastly increase efficiency in the use of national resources.

The Need for Further Development of the Securities Market

Securities markets can play a critical role in raising Lithuania's level of efficiency, for three main reasons. First, they can provide the necessary marketplace for the privatization and pension reform envisaged in these Policy Notes. It is in this market that the sale of state assets will generally take place, and here that the new cohort of savers will seek investment instruments. Second, efficient securities markets, in their own right, can dramatically increase the effectiveness of corporate governance, especially through institutional (domestic and foreign) investors. And third, the markets supply a means of accumulating and allocating capital for productive and relatively long-term and high-risk purposes, an activity that complements the role of banks in their customary financing of shorter maturities and lower risks (especially in transition economies).

Lithuania's securities markets, particularly its stock market, were established anew soon after independence, and the stock market has developed substantially since the process of market transition began (its total capitalization is now equivalent to about one-fifth of GDP). The authorities have succeeded in setting up a relatively efficient and transparent stock exchange, as well as an effective regulatory institution. The market, however, remains marked by its original driving force—mass privatization. This created some 1,500 publicly held companies and about 1.5 million domestic shareholders (about 40 percent of the population) in a very short time. Only about 100 of those companies, however, have annual sales in excess of US$10 million; only some 600 are listed on the stock exchange; just 54 prepared accounts (and had them audited) according to international standards for 1997; and in that year, about US$90 million was invested in the market by domestic, nonbank sources.

8. See J. De Fourgerolles, "Pension Privatization in Latin America: Lessons for Central and Eastern Europe," in *Institute for East-West Studies, Occasional Paper Series* (New York, 1995); and R. Holzmann, "On Economic Benefits and Fiscal Requirements of Moving from Unfunded to Funded Pensions," *European Economy* (forthcoming).

In other words, the market is still relatively small, illiquid, narrow, and most new investments come from abroad; intermediation is highly concentrated; and nonbrokerage intermediation is very limited. While the authorities have made tremendous progress in setting up the right framework for the securities market to develop, several constraints still need to be removed, especially if that market is to provide efficient support to the acceleration of the privatization process and the reform of the pension system.

First, information disclosure remains inadequate. Legally sanctioned domestic accounting and auditing standards along international lines are lacking (a critical issue raised elsewhere in this report); requirements to disclose nonfinancial price-sensitive information are not strictly enforced. Second, the legal mechanisms for shareholders to put performance pressure on managers are weak (again, as discussed previously in this report). In particular, the laws do not carry explicit provisions to force company managers to act in the interest of *all* shareholders—nor do they include clearly defined procedures for calling general shareholder meetings and soliciting proxies, properly specified rules for takeover bids (such as the rights and obligations of the involved parties), or sufficient listing prohibitions for companies with internal regulations that restrict the trading of their shares outside the existing group of shareholders (hampering the emergence of outside, substantial minority owners).

Third, legal constraints also hinder the emergence of institutional investors. On the one hand, the legal framework for voluntary private funding of pensions (and associated pension funds) is still under design, and broader reform of the existing pay-as-you-go system is pending (as explained earlier). On the other hand, the law both openly discriminates against investment companies (unit trusts or mutual funds) by not granting them the tax exemption on income and capital gains from financial assets given to individuals, and effectively prohibits existing intermediaries from adopting multiple roles as brokers, dealers, investment managers, and financial advisers (even under appropriate conflict-of-interest rules).

Finally, privatization and pension reform will tax the operational capacity of the securities market. Privatization could bring between fifteen and thirty major new quality issues to the primary market (and a badly needed breadth to the secondary one) in three years. In the same period, pension reform could increase the demand for securities by up to 30 percent of the current market capitalization.[9] The institutional mechanisms needed to coordinate this three-legged reform (privatization, pensions, and securities market), however, are currently nonexistent beyond informal and occasional contacts among civil servants.

Also, two critical legal deficiencies may limit the benefits (and the very possibility) of faster privatization in—and through—the securities markets. The existing Law on Public Trading of Securities, as it currently stands, may exempt securities issued as part of the cash privatization program from the application of the law (disclosure and investor protection provisions, among other regulations, would not apply to those securities), and the Civil Code provides no clear definition of nominee ownership (a major deterrent to foreign institutional investors who face strict rules on local custodians in their home countries).

A Policy Action Plan for Sustainable, Rapid Growth

In light of the analysis summarized above, and in spite of the many positive reform efforts already implemented, there is little doubt that achieving rapid, sustainable growth in Lithuania will be a

---

9. The experiences of Argentina and Chile illustrate this potential. If not properly implemented, however, this program could seriously alter the stability of, and the public trust in, the securities market, and thus waste an excellent opportunity to develop that market.

demanding undertaking. Policy action is needed on many fronts spread across several branches of government. Implementation will need strong coordination and continuing commitment. Prioritization is crucial, and piecemeal reforms are unlikely to suffice.

The recommendations in this report are thus designed to balance limited implementation capacity with policy comprehensiveness. For that purpose, a phased Policy Action Plan is used, which covers key sectors according to short-, medium-, and long-run priorities. With few exceptions, all the recommended policies could be in place within five years.

It is important to emphasize that while the above-mentioned plan is geared toward the objective of fast and sustainable growth, its implementation will greatly facilitate (if not be a necessary condition for) the country's integration into, and profiting from, the EU

The core of the reform strategy in each area is explained below. The detailed Policy Action Plan is presented in tables 1, 2, and 3 (short-, medium-, and long-term priorities, respectively). A description of what the Lithuanian economy will look like from a macro point of view over the next decade if that plan is applied, and if it is not, is provided in the subsequent section.

Banking

One overriding objective dominates the recommended policy actions—to change the role of the state in banking from owner to regulator. This calls for full and immediate disinvestment (through privatization or, when necessary, closure), but also for the permanent severance of all channels of undue political interference. Amendments to law are urgently needed to make BoL truly independent from Seimas; to undo regulatory privileges for state-controlled banks; and to make the placement of the state's funds, debt, targeted lending programs, and restitution schemes across banks a purely profit-maximizing commercial affair (rather than a tool for banking policy by the government). In the medium-term, key parameters of the deposit insurance system (coverage, assessment, qualification criteria, and the like) should be adjusted to extricate the state from a perceived and potential position of "bank owner and deposit compensator of last resort."

While shifting the effective ownership of the banking industry to the private sector, the authorities should also continue to strengthen the regulatory framework for bank operations (an area in which much has been accomplished over the past two years). In particular, wider and more explicit powers should be granted to BoL in bank resolutions and in gathering information on bank subsidiaries, and to lenders in perfecting and accessing their loan collaterals (among other measures, by allowing banks to own land).

Energy

Converting the state from owner to regulator is a key public policy objective in the energy sector as well. In this area, however, the government faces a critical timing problem. Because of the technical complexities involved (such as functional separations in power), significant time will be required before private entrepreneurs can take ownership of the sector (except for LG, which can and should be immediately privatized). In the meantime, the state-controlled companies concerned have the potential to destabilize central and municipal public finances, to fail to provide vital energy supplies to the economy, or to do both. Ensuring efficiency in the running of companies on their way to privatization (or the emergence of alternative, private sources of supply) is thus critical.

The provision of such assurances will require efficient intervention to facilitate the physical rehabilitation of DH systems, the establishment of fully operational and adequately staffed supervisory boards in all state-controlled energy companies, the unbundling of generation and distribution activities in LPC, and the freedom to articulate performance-related remuneration arrangements for managers, among other measures. Outside the companies themselves, efficiency enhancement should be pursued (and eventual privatization made possible) through the development of an adequate regulatory environment (especially in electricity). This is currently an ongoing effort, but its completion may need to be prioritized. Once a private-sector-led, properly regulated energy sector is in place, the medium-term policy focus should shift toward more effective energy conservation incentives in public procurement, among the energy suppliers themselves, and among large consumers.

Municipal Finance

The accounts of Lithuanian municipalities are excessively volatile, something that seriously hampers their sustainability. Much of that volatility is generated by policy distortions. Removing those distortions is, at this stage, a critical priority for the economy as a whole. Action is needed in three areas. First, expenditure responsibilities need to be immediately clarified between the central and the local government in the matter of unfunded mandates, general investment responsibilities, and the forthcoming cost of rehabilitating the newly decentralized DH system. Second, revenue predictability should be enhanced by granting municipalities greater autonomy to introduce new taxes or tax surcharges (within limits) and by setting key formula parameters for tax sharing and transfers for longer periods (possibly three years). Third, municipal borrowing should be both regulated (through tight debt-service ceilings, central government approvals, information disclosure and auditing requirements, and automatic central government intervention rights in case of defaults) and facilitated (in the short term, this should take the form of a transitional municipal credit facility based on a "hard credit" approach, to be closed or privatized within five years).

Considerable medium-term adjustments should also be made to the system of transfers to eliminate the remaining perverse incentives against collection effort (for instance, "Window One" should be eliminated). Also in the medium term, a new Municipal Budget Law should be enacted to overhaul the way local budgets are drawn up (at present, from an expenditure-need perspective), executed, and supervised.

Agriculture

Although this sector is still midway in the transition process, it will soon face the formidable competition implied by EU pre-integration. This poses a core policy question: how to elicit a rapid efficiency enhancement through restructuring without exacerbating the associated social costs beyond the point of political sustainability. While the full rationalization (and eventual elimination) of market support interventions will likely be achievable only over the medium (and long) run, there are other areas where immediate policy action can deliver important increases in the sector's competitiveness without causing major social dislocation. Chief among these are completion of the land restitution and land privatization processes (a closing deadline for the submission of new claims is imperative, as is the right of Lithuanian legal entities to own land) and disposal of the state's remaining shares in agro-industry.

In parallel, the government needs to begin immediately to prepare itself for the rural development challenge that agricultural restructuring will bring about. Apart from upgrades in rural physical infrastructure (conspicuously neglected during the Soviet years), the emergence of rural financial infrastructure and the retraining of a large part of the farming labor force will need to be facilitated (and, in some cases, funded). This will also bring about the need for change in the capabilities of the civil service institutions that support agriculture toward better provision of technical and market information services.

Privatization

A complete reengineering of individual and institutional incentives is needed in Lithuania's privatization process. At a minimum, the law needs to specify explicitly, and in aggregate terms, what is to be sold, by whom, and when. If it is not possible to revise the law in the short term, the government needs to be specific in specifying what state-owned enterprises and holdings it wishes privatized, how it believes they should be privatized, and in what time-frame this should be achieved. The government will also need to require the use of best privatization practices—including those of market valuations; the recourse to internationally reputed advisers; and transparent, modern sales techniques. Otherwise, privatization will remain a protracted and episodic phenomenon, driven by ad hoc political expediency, rather than by a systematic effort to transfer the ownership of national resources to the private sector as soon as possible. While a central, ministry-level institution with the sole and exclusive mandate and authority to divest public assets as rapidly as possible has been found to be the most effective arrangement from experiences in other countries, the State Property Fund and the Privatization Commission, with strong government support and direction, may be able to move privatization forward effectively over the short term. Nevertheless, the country still needs a privatization champion, which should have (and given the right incentives, will seek to have) at its disposal an ample battery of best-practice privatization tools, including those needed for valuation and sale, and adequate funding to hire needed advisers. In parallel, to make privatization feasible in infrastructure (a promising undertaking), a thorough review of privatization and concession possibilities; economywide and sectoral overlappings in regulation; and the capacities, autonomy, and independence of relevant regulatory institutions will be needed, followed by the implementation of a suitable action plan.

PSD Environment: Tax Administration

Lithuania has enough accumulated technical experience to provide, in a relatively short period of time, a more efficient, transparent, and equitable tax administration, one that could facilitate (rather than constrain) private sector growth and, *at the same time*, gather greater revenues for the fiscal budget. The key in this effort is to make the system much less arbitrary. This can be achieved by immediately establishing an efficient and independent tax appeal tribunal and enacting legally sanctioned systems of accounting and auditing standards aligned with international practices (a critical measure that is also recommended in other areas covered by this report). In the medium term, the system should move to fully adopt a voluntary compliance strategy, to be implemented through a battery of policies that would, in essence, turn the administration into a service, rather than a obstacle, to the taxpayer (by providing assistance to bona fide taxpayers, for example). Less arbitrariness should be accompanied by greater internal efficiency on the part of the tax-related agencies. The introduction of a unique tax identification number (for tax, customs, and social insurance purposes); the reduction in, and centralization of, the number of tax offices; a switch to selective rather than universal auditing; and the eventual integration of the tax, customs, and social security administrations should spearhead that efficiency enhancement.

PSD Environment: The Commercial Judicial System

Judicial reform in Lithuania has so far proceeded on the premise that the judiciary itself cannot manage the adjustments needed to improve the quality of court services. This report recommends a different approach: grant the judiciary full independence, but provide it with the incentives and tools to enhance its own performance. Specifically, responsibility for the budget (but not for its appropriation) and personnel (including appointments and dismissals) of the court system should be given to an independent Court Administration Agency, governed by a board that includes representation of the Ministry of Justice, but is not controlled by it. The agency should then immediately launch a renewed initiative to develop the judges' skills (especially in commercial matters, and with priority given to bankruptcy law); standardize the legislative process (especially at the drafting and quality control stages); and provide better access to justice (replacing revenue-maximizing pricing with a system of cost-based flat rates backed by a legal aid program). Later on, focus should shift toward upgrading the physical infrastructure of the court system (computarization of case assignment and case management, introduction of tape recording of proceedings, automation of court transcripts, electronic access to jurisprudence, and the like) and promoting the use of alternative dispute resolution mechanisms.

PSD Environment: Corporate Governance

The power of shareholders (and, to a lesser extent, banks) as a source of efficiency enhancement remains largely untapped in Lithuania, and relatively simple policy changes can set that power free. First, it is difficult to see how Lithuanian shareholders (or banks) can assess company performance with even the slightest accuracy under current accounting and auditing practices. As recommended in other areas, it is critical that Lithuania adopt a legally sanctioned system of accounting and auditing standards along international lines; that it place the (self-) regulation of those standards in the hands of the profession; and that, for a transitional period, it competitively allocate public funds for the training of accountants and auditors. Second, the Company Law should explicitly provide for a manager's "duty of loyalty" (and penalties for its infringement); for single external boards under nonexecutive control; and for a fuller range of management incentive contracts. Third, the regulatory environment for banks should encourage their participation in the boards of large corporate borrowers (possibly through slightly lower provisioning requirements). Finally, it should be made possible to file complains with the Seimas' Ombudsman against the managers of state-controlled enterprises.

Pension Reform

A three-step approach is proposed. First, the long-term financial viability of the existing pay-as-you-go pension system must be immediately protected. Policies to achieve that objective have already been designed and await implementation. Most critical among them is the acceleration in the rate of increase in retirement ages (to six months annually for both men and women) until they reach sixty-five years (again, for both genders). Second, workers must be presented with undistorted saving and employment signals as soon as possible. Nominally shifting half of the pension contributions from employers to employees, and enhancing, among others, benefit-reporting mechanisms, would convey those kinds of signals. Finally, but perhaps most critical, Lithuania cannot afford to continue forgoing between 0.5 and 1.0 percent of economic growth each year, simply because of the way its people are compelled to save for their retirement. A voluntary "opt-out" clause should be gradually phased into the system to allow workers to divert an increasing part of their pension contribution into privately funded pension accounts. This will create transitional costs for the fiscal budget, but these costs are both worth paying (given expected economywide benefits) and payable (through a conservative combination of modest amounts of debt, higher VAT rates, slight increases in contribution rates, and less generous indexation policies).

Securities Market

Two roles are envisaged in this Action Plan for the securities markets—that it serve as a nexus between privatization and pension reform and as a self-standing, powerful stimulus to the efficient management of companies. The basic legal, regulatory, and institutional frameworks for the market to play those roles are in place. What remains to be done is relatively simple, albeit critical. Simultaneous policy intervention is needed on three fronts. First, an improvement in the channels for information transmission (mainly through better accounting and auditing standards, as recommended elsewhere, and stricter enforcement rules to disclose price-sensitive information) is needed. Second, the obstacles to the emergence of active shareholders must be removed (through more adequate voting rules, better-specified takeover regulations, further disincentives to restrictions on the transferability of shares, and the like). And third, laws and institutions need to be adjusted to handle privatization-related operations in an orderly fashion (for instance, through the provision for nominee ownership in the Civil Code and the establishment of an interagency coordination group).

The Lithuanian Economy over the Coming Decade, with and without Major Reform

Lithuania's macroeconomic future will be shaped by the implementation of the Policy Action Plan articulated above, or by the failure to do so. Two broad possibilities are analyzed here. The first is mild, piecemeal, and ad hoc policymaking; the second is fundamental, comprehensive, and proactive reform. Both scenarios have been incorporated into a macro-consistent projection framework to follow the expected evolution of the main macro variables.[10] *The core result is a choice between moderate growth that would be heavily dependent on external financing, and high growth with low indebtedness.*

The key factor that drives the scenarios apart is the quantity and efficiency of overall investment. In the moderate growth case, investment grows only slowly, for two reasons. On the one hand, the state fails to eliminate completely the quasi-public sector's deficit and is forced to continue reducing its currently dismal public investment program (down to 2 percent of GDP). On the other hand, private investors find less room to operate (because of slower privatization) in a more difficult business climate (brought about by persistent constraints in the PSD environment), are less confident in the macroeconomic sustainability of the country, and are significantly crowded out by the higher interest rates created by the government's own financing needs. Perhaps more important, that lower level of investment is much less productive, because the mechanisms for efficiency enhancement are not in place (pension and securities market reform, among others). All this costs Lithuania dearly. It forgoes a sustained, real GDP growth rate of 6 percent annually in favor of a sustainable 3 percent annual growth path.

While not stellar, the 3 percent path can be regarded as quite satisfactory and is certainly no reason for alarm. It does, however, carry several undesirable features that could permanently mark the Lithuanian economy and hamper the country's regional and EU aspirations. First, Lithuania would remain a place of lingering high inflation (at around 18 percent annually), rather than moving to western European standards of price stability, primarily because of high and continuing fiscal deficits (of about 4–5 percent of GDP annually). This, in the post-currency-board era, would lead to a larger nominal devaluation of the litas against trading partners' currencies, with a natural loss of monetary credibility.

Second, the country would remain heavily dependent on foreign borrowing. Instead of enjoying rapidly declining balance of payments current account deficits (reaching about 2 percent of GDP in the

---

10. Our results are derived from a modified version of the World Bank's Revised Minimum Standard Model-Extended (RMSM-X), adapted to Lithuania's circumstances and projected into the year 2007. While the model does not provide for endogenously generated growth patterns (these are judgmentally incorporated), it does allow for a thorough consistency and feasibility check of policies (especially fiscal ones), private investors' plans, and the country's access to external financing.

outer years), as in the high-growth scenario, moderate growth would leave those deficits at around 5 percent of GDP. This is primarily because the missing efficiency enhancements in the moderate-growth case will eventually translate into weaker export competitiveness. The implied external financing needs would be sizable. By the end of the decade, a moderately growing Lithuania would be twice as indebted as a rapidly growing one (that is, total debt to GDP of 42 rather than 20 percent).

Third, the private sector will also remain heavily dependent on borrowing, which will place continuous pressure on the stability of the domestic banking system. Moderate growth means moderate saving rates and a flow-of-funds pattern that leaves limited room for internal financing in the business sector, which would need to borrow more than a tenth of GDP annually (about two-thirds of its investment, rather than one-third, as in the high-growth case), most of it domestically. This, combined with the state's borrowing needs, would push the banking system's loan portfolio to increase by about 8 percent of GDP annually, double the rate of the high-growth path.

Finally, refraining from comprehensive reform at this stage would virtually condemn Lithuanians to living standards that, while slowly improving (real per capita consumption growth of about 2.8 percent annually), will not catch up with those of their western European neighbors. Put differently, at current trends, Lithuania's per capita GNP would take fifty-four years to reach that of Greece (the lowest in the EU), even if Greece had zero real growth throughout the period. The Policy Action Plan presented in this report is an opportunity to cut that period to about twenty years.

Table 1. A Policy Action Plan for Lithuania: Short-Term Priorities

Area/objective	*Recommended policy* *Short-term priorities (within one year)*
BANKING	
Reduce political interference in banking.	• Immediately amend relevant laws to explicitly stipulate that BoL is independent of Seimas; its actions, budget, and personnel policies require no Seimas approval; only BoL has the right (or option) to act to resolve bank-specific issues; Seimas cannot reduce the salary of BoL's chairman once appointed; all BoL employees enjoy the same independence and security as board members; BoL board membership is prohibited to persons who have shareholdings in or represent a bank (or their immediate relatives); selected data and bank information is confidential; and selected supervisory actions are to be determined by less than the entire BoL board.
	• Abolish legal provision that exempts State Commercial and Agricultural Bank from BoL regulations, as well as the imposition of limits on staff and management compensation in BoL and state-controlled banks.
	• Adopt regulations that prohibit the placement of government funds in banks that do not meet, at a minimum, all BoL prudential standards; establish a bidding mechanism for government deposits; avoid government deposit concentration; and require collateralization for large government deposits.
	• Limit the participation of state-controlled banks in TB auctions to noncompetitive bids.
	• Allow all banks to bid to service, in purely commercial terms, the government's targeted lending and restitution programs.
	• Prohibit borrowing from state-controlled banks to finance restitution programs (even when collateralized).

Area/objective	*Short-term priorities (within one year)*
BANKING (continued)	
Withdraw the state as owner from the banking industry.	• Sell all government and state-enterprise minority stocks in the banking industry.
	• Conclude privatization of Agricultural Bank.
	• Develop a detailed plan for privatizing Savings Bank.
Complete the reform in the legal and regulatory environment of banks.	• Incorporate a definition of insolvency, including the inability to meet liquidity demands, into the law that will permit BoL to close a bank.
	• Incorporate special bankruptcy provision for banks into the Commercial Banking Law to allow for expedited resolution.
	• Introduce explicit provisions in the Commercial Banking Law to explicitly allow for BoL to regulate and examine bank subsidiaries, and to require consolidated accounts.
	• Amend all necessary laws to make temporary bank administrators accountable to BoL, and to give BoL the right to dismiss them.
	• Establish currently envisioned collateral registries and price their services on a cost-recovery (rather than taxing) basis, and adopt necessary laws to allow lenders to automatically seize collateral in case of default and secure the right of creditors (with judicial consent) to recover their collateral from the bankruptcy process.
	• Implement law allowing banks (and all legal entities) to own land.

Area/objective	Recommended policy
	Short-term priorities (within one year)
ENERGY	
Convey a clear signal of the government's policy objectives in the energy sector.	• Adopt a new, time-bound Plan of Action along the lines of the Plan of Action appended to the 1994 Statement of Energy Policy and Strategy, but in recognition of the changes in circumstances over the past four years, incorporate a different emphasis. The new plan should (i) set a date for completion of the regulatory framework for the energy sector, with the necessary agencies staffed, resourced, and at work; (ii) state how a competitive electricity market will operate; (iii) provide a firm schedule for the unbundling of LPC into transparent corporate entities; (iv) provide a firm schedule for the privatization of all the state's investments in the energy sector (except INPP); (v) set out comprehensive governance rules for energy enterprises controlled by the state or by municipalities and specify the duties, prerogatives, and membership guidelines for supervisory boards of such enterprises; and (vi) set targets for energy conservation, for the diversification of energy sources, and for the exploitation of renewable energy resources and proclaim the measures (including incentives and sanctions) being taken to achieve the targets. The new statement should include goals than can be monitored, such as reduction in the economy's energy intensity by 10 percent annually, reduction in the import dependency by 10 percent by the year 2000, reduction in the proportion of oil supplies sourced from any single country to less than 80 percent by 2000, phasing out of consumer subsidies for heat over three years, annual dividend earnings from remaining state-owned energy companies equivalent to 5 percent of net assets, and increasing the private sector share of total electricity generation to 5 percent by 1999.
Assure efficiency and financial stability among newly decentralized district heating (DH) enterprises.	• Carry out study of the investment needs in DH on a municipality-by-municipality basis (an urgent matter). Negotiate and coordinate a borrowing program to obtain the necessary finance to implement a DH rehabilitation effort, concentrating on projects that yield the best combination of economic and environmental benefits. Establishment of a purpose-built transitional municipal credit facility for DH rehabilitation to broker funds to municipalities and DH companies that meet high standards of efficiency and governance is a possibility.
	• Make permanent the provisions that are currently being applied on an effective temporary basis to compel state budgetary organizations to pay their DH bills promptly.
	• Specify through legislation the structure of governance to be applied to DH entities, including the powers and membership of boards. These should have a majority of outside, nonmanagerial representation (such as consumers, financial experts, and business people, as well as representatives of the municipalities).

Area/objective	Recommended policy Short-term priorities (within one year)
ENERGY (continued) Assure efficiency and financial stability among newly decentralized district heating (DH) enterprises (continued).	• Publish regular "league tables" ranking DH entities by their performance on a range of indicators, including profit ratios, tariffs, cost per customer, market share in their areas, heat losses, thermal efficiency, receivables overdue, use of indigenous and renewable fuels, and the like. • Set a deadline for the freeing of heating prices from regulation. This process should proceed in tandem with the introduction of private capital, on an unrestricted basis, to the DH sector.
Establish an adequate regulatory structure for the electricity market.	• Complete the current review of the regulatory environment for energy with a view to establishing a single, fully resourced, and comprehensive regulatory agency that will be responsible for all key issues, such as the licensing of operators and the specification and monitoring of supply standards (in addition to the EPC's existing role in the tariff area). • Following full analysis of options, and in conformity with EU policies, put in place electricity market mechanisms that will provide for competition between, and fair remuneration of, electricity generators, whether the assets under their control are characterized as base load, peak load, or reserve capacity, for efficient bulk trading with distribution utilities, and long-run minimization of the cost of electricity to consumers.
Assure efficient performance in LPC on the way to its privatization.	• Establish each of LPC's remaining generating stations as a separate, state-owned company, its shares controlled by the Ministry of Economy and reporting directly (through its board) to that ministry, until privatization takes place. • Establish each of LPC's seven regional electricity distribution utilities as a separate subsidiary of LPC, incorporated under companies legislation and with municipal representation on its supervisory board—again, until privatization takes place. • Remove all barriers to fully commercial operation in LPC, in particular by replacing the members of the present supervisory board with a board of seven to nine persons, including one executive of the company (the general director), one civil servant, and five to seven others who might include a private sector businessperson, a banker, a financial expert, a consumer, an economist, and an LPC employee elected by the workforce. All of these would be appointed and accountable to the ministry, but their responsibility on the board would be to ensure the highest possible standards of efficiency, service, and financial performance.

Area/objective	Recommended policy Short-term priorities (within one year)
ENERGY (continued)	
Assure efficient performance in LPC on the way to its privatization (continued).	• Appoint boards selected along similar lines to the generating and distribution companies. • Establish a series of performance indicators for achievement by LPC. • Remove all obstacles, such as the current provision that the maximum salary in LPC may not exceed five times the average pay in the company, to the establishment of performance-related remuneration of energy sector managers in line with the compensation provided to managers carrying similar responsibility in the Lithuanian private sector.
Begin to withdraw the state as owner from the power and gas industries.	• Engage experienced, international financial advisers to attract private capital into the electricity industry and to develop a plan for the ultimate privatization of the generation and distribution/supply sectors (the transmission activity, the National Grid, should remain in public ownership). • Immediately place the total privatization of LG in the hands of duly selected international advisers. Assuming that the regulatory agency is in place before the sale is concluded, there should be no need for the government to retain a "golden share." In the meantime, appoint a supervisory board along the lines described above for LPC.
Begin to capture the benefits of energy conservation.	• Provide previously committed (Lt 10 million) funding to the Energy Saving Fund. • Enhance (and provide funding for) the Energy Conservation Program's public education effort. • Include energy-saving technology among criteria for public procurement. • Make the speed of replacement of energy-wasteful equipment and methods in state and municipal energy companies a performance criterion for their supervisory boards.

Area/objective	Recommended policy Short-term priorities (within one year)
MUNICIPAL FINANCE	
Clarify expenditure assignments.	• Immediately discontinue the central government's practice of imposing unfunded mandates on municipalities • Allow municipalities to assume full responsibility for all investments related to the services they provide, whether they exceed Lt 5 million or not. If necessary, until adequate credit markets develop, channel required central financing through matching, conditional, or categorical grants. • Address the financial and operational problems of DH companies (see above).
Achieve much higher levels of revenue certainty.	• Decouple the financing of the Health Insurance Fund from revenue sharings (and fund it through the central government budget). • Set personal income tax sharing rates as well as parameters in the new system of equalization transfers for a period of three years (instead of one, as at present). • Enhance revenue autonomy among municipalities by introducing taxes that are exclusively assigned to local governments (giving them the discretion to vary rates within predetermined bands; candidates would be real estate and motor vehicle taxes and/or surtaxes on PIT, with some discretion over rates).
Provide an efficient and conservative framework for municipal borrowing.	• Regulate long-term municipal borrowing to allow its use only for capital investment purposes, under strict limits (for example, long-term debt service should not exceed 15 percent of recurrent revenues), for the aggregate of debt and debt guarantees, with prior approval by the Ministry of Finance (in case of international borrowing) and under comprehensive reporting and yearly auditing requirements (a public debt registry of local government debt should be maintained). • Short-term borrowing for liquidity management should only be allowed if it does not exceed 5 percent of projected revenues and should be repaid at year-end.

Area/objective	Recommended policy Short-term priorities (within one year)
MUNICIPAL FINANCE (continued) Facilitate the development of credit sources for municipalities and municipal companies.	• Establish a transitional municipal credit facility to lend directly to municipalities and municipal enterprises with a strict "hard credit" approach.
AGRICULTURE Complete the land restitution and land privatization process.	• Continue to accelerate land restitution and titling, and increase incentives for claimants to accept compensation instead of land. • Allow legal entities to own agricultural land.
Complete the privatization of agricultural companies.	• Speed up privatization of the remaining state shares in agro-industry, especially minority holdings.
Meet the challenge of integrated rural development.	• Amend legislation to permit greater use of the forms of collateral generally available in rural areas, such as farm real estate, farm equipment, inventory, accounts receivable, warehouse receipts, and consumer goods. Improve access to public collateral registries in rural areas, especially for moveable property. Establish publicly funded, privately delivered rural credit bureaus to facilitate screening of credit applicants. • Initiate a pilot demonstration experiment to bring retail banking to rural areas. • Design and begin implementing a publicly funded, privately delivered rural retraining program to prepare farmers and farm workers to compete in growing sectors of the labor market.

27

Area/objective	Short-term priorities (within one year)
PRIVATIZATION	
Build a clear legal and institutional framework for privatization with built-in incentives to sell.	• Enact new privatization law to set forth, inter alia, the overall goals of privatization (disinvestment rather than revenue collection); what is to be sold (both companies in the tradable and infrastructure areas should be included) in aggregate terms, and by what time; the creation of a central Ministry of Privatization (incorporating the existing Privatization Commission and Privatization Agency), which will be exclusively and solely responsible for selling state-owned assets and will have wide authority to use best practices (especially valuation methods) and adequate funding; the immediate transfer of all sale proceeds to the fiscal budget (except for those used to pay sale costs); and high standards of disclosure and transparency. If it is not feasible for the government to revise the current law and privatization institutional structure in the short term, the government should provide specific instructions annually on what state-owned enterprises or holdings should be privatized, indicating what sales methods are preferred and providing time frames. The privatization institutions should be provided with adequate funding, political support, and instructions so that needed advisers can be hired and best practices used. The use of modern, transparent sales techniques should be a key requirement.
Make a new battery of privatization tools available.	• The new privatization law, or instructions given the privatization institutions (see above), should explicitly require the use of all sales methods, including public offerings, trade (third-party) sales, mixed sales, negotiated sales, and flexible disposal mechanisms (such as packaging shares) for leftover minority holdings in small and medium-size enterprises.
Facilitate infrastructure privatization.	• In conjunction with the public investment program, identify a list of suitable cases for the application of the powers granted by the Concession Law. Engage (possibly through the new Ministry of Privatization) experienced advisers to market and implement those concession opportunities.
	• Review the consistency between economywide and sector-specific competition rules (for example, access to networks versus abuse of dominant market position); among infrastructure-related regulators, sector ministries, and economywide regulators; and between sectoral regulation needs in the post-privatization era and the institutional capacity of existing agencies. Implement an action plan to remove eventual inconsistencies.

Area/objective	Recommended policy Short-term priorities (within one year)
PRIVATIZATION (continued)	
Facilitate infrastructure privatization (continued).	• To increase regulatory independence, remove the telecommunications regulatory functions from the Ministry of Communications; eliminate budget funding of regulatory bodies and replace it with earmarked funding; increase the autonomy of the Competition Agency; and ensure that members of the Energy Commission are allowed to serve full terms unless professional incompetence or illegal behavior can be demonstrated.
TAX ADMINISTRATION	
Eliminate arbitrariness.	• Establish an efficient, independent tax appeal tribunal. Enact a legally sanctioned system of accounting and auditing standards (aligned with international standards).
Improve the internal efficiency of the tax administration agencies.	• Establish a centralized and unique tax identification number for all taxes, customs duties, and social security contributions. Abandon universal auditing system and replace it with selective auditing mechanisms. Eliminate lags between assessment and collection. Introduce a minimum tax for both incorporated and unincorporated businesses, with explicit guidelines for presumptive taxation of hard-to-tax groups.
COMMERCIAL JUDICIAL SYSTEM	
Enhance the independence of the judiciary.	• Establish a Court Administration Agency, governed by a board with representation—but not control—by the Ministry of Justice, to be in charge of the budget (albeit not the appropriation) and the administration of the court system. The agency should, among other things, also be in charge of staff policy, including appointments, promotion, training, and dismissals. The Ministry of Justice should continue having responsibility for the inspection and audit of the business and the financial activities of the courts.
Improve the legislative process.	• Standardize the process of drafting and enacting laws, with obligatory appointment of single, time-bound, broadly participatory preparation committees (which should include representation of the future law's consumers) and with a unified "quality control" mechanism for language, practical applicability, and conformity with existing legislation under the Ministry of Justice (if possible).

29

Area/objective	Recommended policy *Short-term priorities (within one year)*
COMMERCIAL JUDICIAL SYSTEM (continued)	
Upgrade the skills of judges and other court personnel.	• **Provide necessary funding for the Lithuanian Judicial Training Center to enlarge its training curricula in commercial matters (especially bankruptcy, contract law, intellectual property legislation, and financial legislation) under the supervision of the Supreme Court and the Judges' Association, not the Ministry of Justice.** • **Delegate the administration of the judge traineeship system (and of confirming final appointments) to the proposed Court Administration Agency.** • **Institute a comprehensive code of ethics, to be drafted and enforced by the Judges' Association.**
Achieve better access to justice.	• **Replace the current fee system (proportion of value of claim, payable up front) with a cost-recovering (rather than revenue maximizing) flat rate. Enforce the loser-pays-costs principle.** • **Establish a publicly funded, means-tested legal assistance program for the neediest commercial users (such as microentrepreneurs), to be administered by the proposed Court Administration Agency.**
CORPORATE GOVERNANCE *(see also recommendations under Securities Markets, Banking, Privatization, and Pension Reform).*	
Improve legal protection of investors.	• **Amend the Company Law to establish the managers' "duty of loyalty" to shareholders, and the penalties for failure in that duty.** • **Enact accounting and auditing laws that meet international standards and EU directives, and make those standards legally applicable to financial statements for tax purposes (and binding for tax collectors). Reconstitute the board of the Lithuanian Accounting Institute to put majority control in the hands of private professionals, and make the institute the regulatory body for those laws (as a first step toward self-regulation by the profession). As a temporary measure, competitively allocate government funds to the Institute and to other private suppliers for the appropriate training of accountants and auditors in keeping with the new standards set by the previously mentioned laws.**

Area/objective	Recommended policy Short-term priorities (within one year)
CORPORATE GOVERNANCE (continued) *(see also recommendations under Securities Markets, Banking, Privatization, and Pension Reform).*	
Facilitate the role of banks in corporate governance.	• Review regulatory environment for banks to identify and implement possible incentives for banks to include board representation clauses in large lending contracts (for example, by slightly lower provisioning requirements for such loans).
Facilitate board-management interaction.	• Amend the Company Law to introduce governance systems with only one external board, which would have at least a majority of nonexecutive members, with only nonexecutive members eligible to be chairman. Board members' fees would be payable as normal business expenses (not exclusively out of profits). Include legal provisions governing a full range of management incentives (stock options, warrants, and the like).
Facilitate mechanisms for corporate governance among state-controlled enterprises.	• In addition to the privatization-specific recommendations described above, amend the legal framework for the operation of the Office of Seimas' Ombudsman to allow for the filing of complaints against public enterprise managers (as part of the civil service), filing by foreign individual and institutional investors operating in Lithuania, and a broader range of penalties for failure to disclose information to the Ombudsman.

Area/objective	Recommended policy *Short-term priorities (within one year)*
PENSION SYSTEM	
Assure long-term fiscal viability of the current system.	• Accelerate the annual rate of increase in the retirement age to six months for both men and women until the retirement age of sixty-five is reached for both genders. Sever the link between the years-of-service flat benefit component and the minimum standard of living index. Change the indexation mechanism of the supplementary pension to reflect the envelope of available resources.
Improve labor market incentives and other improvements to Paygo system.	• Shift 11 percentage points of the 22.5 percent payroll contribution rate to employees, with a mandatory and commensurate increase in wages to leave workers with the same level of post-contribution income; introduce periodic reporting of contributions and benefits. • Provide for continued accruals after thirty years in the basic pension; reexamine actuarial adjustments for delayed retirement. • Enact draft legislation for private (nonstate) pensions and develop plan to implement law.
SECURITIES MARKET *(see also Corporate Governance)*	
Improve the quality of market information transmission mechanisms.	• Following the legal enactment of new accounting and auditing standards along international lines (as described under Corporate Governance), require all listed companies to meet those standards (or be removed from the list). • Enforce current rules for disclosure of price-sensitive information and amend the Securities Market Law to include explicit requirements for "continuous" disclosure of price-sensitive information by listed companies.

Area/objective	Recommended policy *Short-term priorities (within one year)*
SECURITIES MARKET (continued) (*see also Corporate Governance*) Facilitate the emergence of "active" shareholders.	• Amend the Company Law and the Securities Market Law to detail the procedures for calling general meetings, soliciting proxies, and voting with proxies, as well as the triggering events and processes that allow takeovers to occur (and the rights and obligations of the parties involved in the takeover). • Prohibit companies with self-imposed restrictions on share transfers from listing in the NSEL. • Exempt authorized investment companies that act only as pass-through investment vehicles from the 28 percent profit tax (with a view to giving the same tax treatment to all investment instruments). • Amend the Investment Companies Law to replace the prohibition on related-party activities with a detailed set of conflict-of-interest provisions and an explicit duty of managers to act in the best interest of clients.
Assure the operational absorptive capacity of the securities market to support privatization and pension reform.	• If necessary, amend the Law on Public Trading of Securities so that the private placement of securities under cash privatization is exempted from the full-prospectus disclosure requirements of NSEL. The law, however, should fully apply to securities floated in the market under the privatization program. • Amend the Civil Code to provide a clear definition of the concept of nominee ownership (especially in regard to local custodian services). • Establish an interagency coordinating committee to identify, on an ongoing basis, any emerging constraints to privatization and pension reform related to the securities market and to propose, plan, and implement necessary remedial actions.

33

Table 2. A Policy Action Plan for Lithuania: Medium-Term Priorities

Area/objective	Recommended policy Medium-term priorities (within three years)
BANKING	
Withdraw the state as owner from the banking industry.	• Conclude the privatization of Savings Bank.
Complete the reform of the legal and regulatory environment of banks.	• Combine the laws that regulate banks into a single statute. • Codify penalties and fines for financial crimes involving banks, including appeals procedures, in the Banking Law. • Adopt laws to allow syndicated lending, both within and outside the banking system.
Rationalize the deposit insurance scheme.	• Amend the level of deposit insurance protection to ensure that it is not excessive for Lithuania (Lt 10,000 would cover 98 percent of individual deposits). Do not impose overburdening assessments on participatory banks, and ensure that coinsurance levels for foreign currencies meet EU standards. Allow the Deposit Insurance Fund to reduce assessments if the targeted minimum level of funding is achieved. • Give the Deposit Insurance Fund the right to file claims in bankruptcy proceedings to recover money advanced to pay depositors, to be appointed administrator for the bankrupt estate, and to manage the asset resolution.
ENERGY	
Withdraw the state as owner from the power and gas industries.	• Sell-off the state's assets in electricity generation and distribution. • Fully privatize LG.

Area/objective	Recommended policy Medium-term priorities (within three years)
ENERGY (continued)	
Capture the benefits of energy conservation.	• Enact legislation requiring energy audits from large industrial, commercial, and institutional consumers.
MUNICIPAL FINANCE	
Remove remaining perverse incentives against revenue mobilization.	• Eliminate "Window One" (reserves for extraordinary events) from the overall system of transfers. • Base equalization transfers under "Window Two" (equalization of tax revenues) on fiscal capacity as approximated by measures of tax bases (rather than forecast or actual collections). • Control for the relative size of the municipalities' populations in "Window Three" (equalization of expenditure needs).
Facilitate the development of credit sources for municipalities and municipal companies.	• Extend the operations of the transitional municipal credit facility to include "loan to lender" and "municipal bond banking."
Improve the budget process at the municipal level.	• Enact a new municipal budget law to provide for the preparation of municipal budgets from a perspective of revenue availability (rather than expenditure need), introduce a modern treasury function for budget execution, introduce budget evaluation systems, and strengthen existing institutions of control and audit.
AGRICULTURE	
Complete the land restitution and land privatization process.	• Sell any remaining land that has not been restituted or claimed by the deadline for new claims.
Complete the privatization of agricultural companies.	• Allow "farmer shares" to enjoy the same trading conditions as other shares in agricultural companies.

Area/objective	Recommended policy Medium-term priorities (within three years)
AGRICULTURE (continued) Complete the rationalization of agriculture support mechanisms.	• Replace the current MMPP system with a very modest, contingent safety net or direct payment program targeted for quality enhancement. • Replace the current, highly distorting sugar market protection mechanisms with fixed, direct payments to farmers based on a transferable quota right that would decline over time.
Meet the challenge of integrated rural development.	• Design and implement a public infrastructure investment program for rural areas that takes into account both the need to attract private capital and to meet the government's social objectives.
Adapt the civil service to the new needs of the post-adjustment agricultural sector.	• Establish agricultural statistics collection mechanisms, a market information dissemination unit, and a policy analysis agency within the new structure of the Ministry of Agriculture.
TAX ADMINISTRATION Eliminate arbitrariness.	• Move to a voluntary compliance system. Issue a "taxpayer charter," appoint a tax-related ombudsman, disseminate regular reports on how tax proceeds are actually used, provide greater assistance to bona fide taxpayers, and establish an early assessment facility.
Improve the internal efficiency of the tax administration agencies.	• Centralize and reduce the number of tax collection offices. Issue (and keep up-to-date) internal staff manuals of current tax laws and their interpretation by the courts and by the central office.

Area/objective	Medium-term priorities (within three years)
COMMERCIAL JUDICIAL SYSTEM	
Enhance the independence of the judiciary.	• Gradually shift responsibility for court procedures to the Court Administration Agency (such as case management; production, maintenance, and dissemination of records, decisions, and jurisprudence; and so forth).
Improve court procedures.	• Computerize court functions, including case assignment and management. • Introduce tape recording of court proceedings and automate the production of court transcripts. • Store court decisions electronically, and make them accessible to judges and the public. • Expand the right of the Supreme Court to publish decisions and interpretations. • Introduce and enforce fines for dilatory tactics. • Overhaul the enterprise register and its supporting law.
CORPORATE GOVERNANCE *(see also recommendations under Securities Markets, Banking, Privatization, and Pension Reform)*	
Facilitate the emergence of large investors.	• Review the status, legislation, and regulation of the insurance sector (both life and property) to identify and remove constraints in the development of a private-sector-led insurance industry.
PENSION SYSTEM	
Capture the efficiency and growth benefits of privately funded pension accounts.	• Provide for a voluntary partial "opt-out" that permits workers to divert some portion of their payroll contribution to private pension accounts, with a commensurate reduction in their accrual of benefits under the earnings-related (supplementary) pension benefit. Phase in the opt-out over time, initially making it available only to workers ten years or more away from retirement, and subject to the constraint that the transition should not be financed solely with debt (except in the very short term), but instead through a combination of a higher VAT rate, a modest increase in the contribution rate, and the indexation of the earnings-related benefit to price inflation, rather than wage growth (or by some combination of the two).

Table 3. A Policy Action Plan for Lithuania: Long-Term Priorities

Area/objective	Recommended policy Long-term priorities (within five years)
ENERGY Capture the benefits of energy conservation.	• Extend energy auditing requirements to all industrial, commercial, and institutional customers.
MUNICIPAL FINANCE Facilitate the development of credit sources for municipalities and municipal companies.	• Close or privatize the transitional municipal credit facility.
AGRICULTURE Complete the rationalization of agricultural support mechanisms.	• Institutionalize a long-term, comprehensive framework for domestic support and foreign trade policy.
TAX ADMINISTRATION Improve the internal efficiency of the tax administration agencies.	• Integrate the tax and customs administrations (together with the existing joint control of VAT and income and profit taxes) with that of social security contributions.
COMMERCIAL JUDICIAL SYSTEM Upgrade the skills of judges and other court personnel.	• Require a period of training (6–12 months) in court before graduation from state-sponsored law schools. Facilitate the development of degree programs for bailiffs, court secretaries, and other court support personnel. • Review the legal and regulatory framework for the establishment and operation of private law schools, with a view to removing any remaining constraints.

Area/objective	Recommended policy Long-term priorities (within five years)
COMMERCIAL JUDICIAL SYSTEM (continued) Foster alternative dispute-resolution mechanisms.	• Amend the Law on Courts to provide for court-associated arbitration mechanisms, including mediation, early neutral evaluation, pretrial conferences, and settlement conferences. • Review the Arbitration Law and the institutional capacity of the government-sponsored Vilnius International Commercial Arbitration Institute, with a view to identifying and removing constraints to the wider use of private arbitration. In coordination with the proposed Court Administration Agency, launch an information campaign to foster the inclusion of private arbitration clauses in commercial contracts. Provide necessary funding to the Judicial Training Center for the training of judges in arbitration techniques.
CORPORATE GOVERNANCE *(see also recommendations under Securities Markets, Banking, Privatization, and Pension Reform)* Facilitate the emergence of large investors.	• Privatize all state ownership in the insurance industry.

39

Distributors of World Bank Publications

Prices and credit terms vary from country to country. Consult your local distributor before placing an order.

ARGENTINA
Oficina del Libro Internacional
Av. Cordoba 1877
1120 Buenos Aires
Tel: (54 11) 815-8354
Fax: (54 11) 815-8156
E-mail: olilibro@satlink.com

**AUSTRALIA, FIJI, PAPUA NEW GUINEA,
SOLOMON ISLANDS, VANUATU, AND
SAMOA**
D.A. Information Services
648 Whitehorse Road
Mitcham 3132
Victoria
Tel: (61) 3 9210 7777
Fax: (61) 3 9210 7788
E-mail: service@dadirect.com.au

AUSTRIA
Gerold and Co.
Weihburggasse 26
A-1011 Wien
Tel: (43 1) 512-47-31-0
Fax: (43 1) 512-47-31-29

BANGLADESH
Micro Industries Development
Assistance Society (MIDAS)
House 5, Road 16
Dhanmondi R/Area
Dhaka 1209
Tel: (880 2) 326427
Fax: (880 2) 811188

BELGIUM
Jean De Lannoy
Av. du Roi 202
1060 Brussels
Tel: (32 2) 538-5169
Fax: (32 2) 538-0841

BRAZIL
Publicações Tecnicas Internacionais Ltda.
Rua Peixoto Gomide, 209
01409 Sao Paulo, SP.
Tel: (55 11) 259-6644
Fax: (55 11) 258-6990
E-mail: postmaster@pti.uol.br

CANADA
Renouf Publishing Co. Ltd.
5369 Canotek Road
Ottawa, Ontario K1J 9J3
Tel: (613) 745-2665
Fax: (613) 745-7660
E-mail: order.dept@renoufbooks.com

CHINA
China Financial & Economic
Publishing House
8, Da Fo Si Dong Jie
Beijing
Tel: (86 10) 6333-8257
Fax: (86 10) 6401-7365

China Book Import Centre
P.O. Box 2825
Beijing

COLOMBIA
Infoenlace Ltda.
Carrera 6 No. 51-21
Apartado Aereo 34270
Santafé de Bogotá, D.C.
Tel: (57 1) 285-2798
Fax: (57 1) 285-2798

COTE D'IVOIRE
Center d'Edition et de Diffusion Africaines
(CEDA)
04 B.P. 541
Abidjan 04
Tel: (225) 24 6510;24 6511
Fax: (225) 25 0567

CYPRUS
Center for Applied Research
Cyprus College
6, Diogenes Street, Engomi
P.O. Box 2006
Nicosia
Tel: (357 2) 44-1730
Fax: (357 2) 46-2051

CZECH REPUBLIC
USIS, NIS Prodejna
Havelkova 22
130 00 Prague 3
Tel: (420 2) 2423 1486
Fax: (420 2) 2423 1114

DENMARK
SamfundsLitteratur
Rosenoerns Allé 11
DK-1970 Frederiksberg C
Tel: (45 31) 351942
Fax: (45 31) 357822

ECUADOR
Libri Mundi
Librería Internacional
P.O. Box 17-01-3029
Juan Leon Mera 851
Quito
Tel: (593 2) 521-606; (593 2) 544-185
Fax: (593 2) 504-209
E-mail: librimu1@librimundi.com.ec

CODEU
Ruiz de Castilla 763, Edif. Expocolor
Primer piso, Of. #2
Quito
Tel/Fax: (593 2) 507-383; 253-091
E-mail: codeu@impsat.net.ec

EGYPT, ARAB REPUBLIC OF
Al Ahram Distribution Agency
Al Galaa Street
Cairo
Tel: (20 2) 578-6083
Fax: (20 2) 578-6833

The Middle East Observer
41, Sherif Street
Cairo
Tel: (20 2) 393-9732
Fax: (20 2) 393-9732

FINLAND
Akateeminen Kirjakauppa
P.O. Box 128
FIN-00101 Helsinki
Tel: (358 0) 121 4418
Fax: (358 0) 121-4435
E-mail: akatilaus@stockmann.fi

FRANCE
World Bank Publications
66, avenue d'Iéna
75116 Paris
Tel: (33 1) 40-69-30-56/57
Fax: (33 1) 40-69-30-68

GERMANY
UNO-Verlag
Poppelsdorfer Allee 55
53115 Bonn
Tel: (49 228) 949020
Fax: (49 228) 217492
E-mail: unoverlag@aol.com

GHANA
Epp Books Services
P.O. Box 44
TUC
Accra

GREECE
Papasotiriou S.A.
35, Stournara Str.
106 82 Athens
Tel: (30 1) 364-1826
Fax: (30 1) 364-8254

HAITI
Culture Diffusion
5, Rue Capois
C.P. 257
Port-au-Prince
Tel: (509) 23 9260
Fax: (509) 23 4858

HONG KONG, CHINA; MACAO
Asia 2000 Ltd.
Sales & Circulation Department
Seabird House, unit 1101-02
22-28 Wyndham Street, Central
Hong Kong
Tel: (852) 2530-1409
Fax: (852) 2526-1107
E-mail: sales@asia2000.com.hk

HUNGARY
Euro Info Service
Margitszgeti Europa Haz
H-1138 Budapest
Tel: (36 1) 350 80 24, 350 80 25
Fax: (36 1) 350 90 32
E-mail: euroinfo@mail.matav.hu

INDIA
Allied Publishers Ltd.
751 Mount Road
Madras - 600 002
Tel: (91 44) 852-3938
Fax: (91 44) 852-0649

INDONESIA
Pt. Indira Limited
Jalan Borobudur 20
P.O. Box 181
Jakarta 10320
Tel: (62 21) 390-4290
Fax: (62 21) 390-4289

IRAN
Ketab Sara Co. Publishers
Khaled Eslamboli Ave., 6th Street
Delafrooz Alley No. 8
P.O. Box 15745-733
Tehran 15117
Tel: (98 21) 8717819; 8716104
Fax: (98 21) 8712479

IRELAND
Government Supplies Agency
Oifig an tSoláthair
4-5 Harcourt Road
Dublin 2
Tel: (353 1) 661-3111
Fax: (353 1) 475-2670

ISRAEL
Yozmot Literature Ltd.
P.O. Box 56055
3 Yohanan Hasandlar Street
Tel Aviv 61560
Tel: (972 3) 5285-397
Fax: (972 3) 5285-397

R.O.Y. International
PO Box 13056
Tel Aviv 61130
Tel: (972 3) 5461423
Fax: (972 3) 5461442
E-mail: royil@netvision.net.il

Palestinian Authority/Middle East
Index Information Services
P.O.B. 19502 Jerusalem
Tel: (972 2) 6271219
Fax: (972 2) 6271634

ITALY
Licosa Commissionaria Sansoni SPA
Via Duca Di Calabria, 1/1
Casella Postale 552
50125 Firenze
Tel: (55) 645-415
Fax: (55) 641-257
E-mail: licosa@ftbcc.it

JAMAICA
Ian Randle Publishers Ltd.
206 Old Hope Road, Kingston 6
Tel: 876-927-2085
Fax: 876-977-0243
E-mail: irpl@colis.com

JAPAN
Eastern Book Service
3-13 Hongo 3-chome, Bunkyo-ku
Tokyo 113
Tel: (81 3) 3818-0861
Fax: (81 3) 3818-0864
E-mail: orders@svt-ebs.co.jp

KENYA
Africa Book Service (E.A.) Ltd.
Quaran House, Mfangano Street
P.O. Box 45245
Nairobi
Tel: (254 2) 223 641
Fax: (254 2) 330 272

KOREA, REPUBLIC OF
Deejon Trading Co. Ltd.
P.O. Box 34, Youida, 706 Seoun Bldg
44-6 Youido-Dong, Yeongchengpo-Ku
Seoul
Tel: (82 2) 785-1631/4
Fax: (82 2) 784-0315

LEBANON
Librairie du Liban
P.O. Box 11-9232
Beirut
Tel: (961 9) 217 944
Fax: (961 9) 217 434

MALAYSIA
University of Malaya Cooperative
Bookshop, Limited
P.O. Box 1127
Jalan Pantai Baru
59700 Kuala Lumpur
Tel: (60 3) 756-5000
Fax: (60 3) 755-4424
E-mail: umkoop@tm.net.my

MEXICO
INFOTEC
Av. San Fernando No. 37
Col. Toriello Guerra
14050 Mexico, D.F.
Tel: (52 5) 624-2800
Fax: (52 5) 624-2822
E-mail: infotec@rtn.net.mx

Mundi-Prensa Mexico S.A. de C.V.
c/Rio Panuco, 141-Colonia Cuauhtemoc
06500 Mexico, D.F.
Tel: (52 5) 533-5658
Fax: (52 5) 514-6799

NEPAL
Everest Media International Services (P) Ltd.
GPO Box 5443
Kathmandu
Tel: (977 1) 472 152
Fax: (977 1) 224 431

NETHERLANDS
De Lindeboom/InOr-Publicaties
P.O. Box 202, 7480 AE Haaksbergen
Tel: (31 53) 574-0004
Fax: (31 53) 572-9296
E-mail: lindeboo@worldonline.nl

NEW ZEALAND
EBSCO NZ Ltd.
Private Mail Bag 99914
New Market
Auckland
Tel: (64 9) 524-8119
Fax: (64 9) 524-8067

NIGERIA
University Press Limited
Three Crowns Building Jericho
Private Mail Bag 5095
Ibadan
Tel: (234 22) 41-1356
Fax: (234 22) 41-2056

NORWAY
NIC Info A/S
Book Department, Postboks 6512 Etterstad
N-0606 Oslo
Tel: (47 22) 97-4500
Fax: (47 22) 97-4545

PAKISTAN
Mirza Book Agency
65, Shahrah-e-Quaid-e-Azam
Lahore 54000
Tel: (92 42) 735 3601
Fax: (92 42) 576 3714

Oxford University Press
5 Bangalore Town
Sharae Faisal
Karachi-75350
Tel: (92 21) 446307
E-mail: ouppak@TheOffice.net

Pak Book Corporation
Aziz Chambers 21, Queen's Road
Lahore
Tel: (92 42) 636 3222; 636 0885
Fax: (92 42) 636 2328
E-mail: pbc@brain.net.pk

PERU
Editorial Desarrollo SA
Apartado 3824, Lima 1
Tel: (51 14) 285380
Fax: (51 14) 286628

PHILIPPINES
International Booksource Center Inc.
1127-A Antipolo St, Barangay, Venezuela
Makati City
Tel: (63 2) 896 6501; 6505; 6507
Fax: (63 2) 896 1741

POLAND
International Publishing Service
Ul. Piekna 31/37
00-677 Warzawa
Tel: (48 2) 628-6089
Fax: (48 2) 621-7255
E-mail: books%ips@ikp.atm.com.pl

PORTUGAL
Livraria Portugal
Apartado 2681, Rua Do Carmo 70-74
1200 Lisbon
Tel: (1) 347-4982
Fax: (1) 347-0264

ROMANIA
Compani De Librarii Bucuresti S.A.
Str. Lipscani no. 26, sector 3
Bucharest
Tel: (40 1) 613 9645
Fax: (40 1) 312 4000

RUSSIAN FEDERATION
Isdatelstvo <Ves Mir>
9a, Kolpachniy Pereulok
Moscow 101831
Tel: (7 095) 917 87 49
Fax: (7 095) 917 92 59

**SINGAPORE; TAIWAN, CHINA;
MYANMAR; BRUNEI**
Ashgate Publishing Asia Pacific Pte. Ltd.
41 Kallang Pudding Road #04-03
Golden Wheel Building
Singapore 349316
Tel: (65) 741-5166
Fax: (65) 742-9356
E-mail: ashgate@asianconnect.com

SLOVENIA
Gospodarski Vestnik Publishing Group
Dunajska cesta 5
1000 Ljubljana
Tel: (386 61) 133 83 47; 132 12 30
Fax: (386 61) 133 80 30
E-mail: repansekj@gvestnik.si

SOUTH AFRICA, BOTSWANA
For single titles:
Oxford University Press Southern Africa
Vasco Boulevard, Goodwood
P.O. Box 12119, N1 City 7463
Cape Town
Tel: (27 21) 595 4400
Fax: (27 21) 595 4430
E-mail: oxford@oup.co.za

For subscription orders:
International Subscription Service
P.O. Box 41095
Craighall
Johannesburg 2024
Tel: (27 11) 880-1448
Fax: (27 11) 880-6248
E-mail: iss@is.co.za

SPAIN
Mundi-Prensa Libros, S.A.
Castello 37
28001 Madrid
Tel: (34 1) 431-3399
Fax: (34 1) 575-3998
E-mail: libreria@mundiprensa.es

Mundi-Prensa Barcelona
Consell de Cent, 391
08009 Barcelona
Tel: (34 3) 488-3492
Fax: (34 3) 487-7659
E-mail: barcelona@mundiprensa.es

SRI LANKA, THE MALDIVES
Lake House Bookshop
100, Sir Chittampalam Gardiner Mawatha
Colombo 2
Tel: (94 1) 32105

Fax: (94 1) 432104
E-mail: LHL@sri.lanka.net

SWEDEN
Wennergren-Williams AB
P.O. Box 1305
S-171 25 Solna
Tel: (46 8) 705-97-50
Fax: (46 8) 27-00-71
E-mail: mail@wwi.se

SWITZERLAND
Librairie Payot Service Institutionnel
Côtes-de-Montbenon 30
1002 Lausanne
Tel: (41 21) 341-3229
Fax: (41 21) 341-3235

ADECO Van Diemen EditionsTechniques
Ch. de Lacuez 41
CH1807 Blonay
Tel: (41 21) 943 2673
Fax: (41 21) 943 3605

THAILAND
Central Books Distribution
306 Silom Road
Bangkok 10500
Tel: (66 2) 235-5400
Fax: (66 2) 237-8321

**TRINIDAD & TOBAGO
AND THE CARRIBBEAN**
Systematics Studies Ltd.
St. Augustine Shopping Center
Eastern Main Road, St. Augustine
Trinidad & Tobago, West Indies
Tel: (868) 645-8467
Fax: (868) 645-8467
E-mail: tobe@trinidad.net

UGANDA
Gustro Ltd.
PO Box 9997, Madhvani Building
Plot 16/4 Jinja Rd.
Kampala
Tel: (256 41) 251 467
Fax: (256 41) 251 468
E-mail: gus@swiftuganda.com

UNITED KINGDOM
Microinfo Ltd.
P.O. Box 3, Alton, Hampshire GU34 2PG
England
Tel: (44 1420) 86848
Fax: (44 1420) 89889
E-mail: wbank@ukminfo.demon.co.uk

The Stationery Office
51 Nine Elms Lane
London SW8 5DR
Tel: (44 171) 873-8400
Fax: (44 171) 873-8242

VENEZUELA
Tecni-Ciencia Libros, S.A.
Centro Cuidad Comercial Tamanco
Nivel C2, Caracas
Tel: (58 2) 959 5547; 5035; 0016
Fax: (58 2) 959 5636

ZAMBIA
University Bookshop, University of Zambia
Great East Road Campus
P.O. Box 32379
Lusaka
Tel: (260 1) 252 576
Fax: (260 1) 253 952

ZIMBABWE
Academic and Baobab Books (Pvt.) Ltd.
4 Conald Road, Granitesde
P.O. Box 567
Harare
Tel: 263 4 755035
Fax: 263 4 781913